POSTWAR INDUSTRIAL POLICY IN JAPAN:

An Annotated Bibliography

by
KARL BOGER

The Scarecrow Press, Inc.

Metuchen, N.J., & London

1988

Library of Congress Cataloging-in-
Publication Data

Boger, Karl.
    Postwar industrial policy in Japan : an
annotated bibliography / by Karl Boger.
        p.   cm.
    Includes indexes.
    ISBN 0-8108-2080-3
    1. Industry and state--Japan--
Bibliography. 2. Japan--Economic policy
--1945- --Bibliography. 3. Japan--Economic
conditions--1945- --Bibliography.   I. Title.
Z7165.J3B63 1988
[HD3616.J33]
016.338952--dc19   87-26535
                                            CIP

TABLE OF CONTENTS

PREFACE

The interest in the United States over industrial
policy stems from the relative economic stagnation of
the last two decades and the overwhelming success of
the Japanese economy in the international marketplace.
In the U.S. domestic market, this has been especially
true of automobiles, semiconductors, computers, and
other "high-tech" products. In a simplistic way this
success can be attributed to the general economic law
of producing quality commodities at low prices. But
what has made this possible for the Japanese and not
for other industrialized economies?

This annotated bibliography provides the
researcher with material to investigate this question
by presenting him/her with writings on Japanese
industrial policy in the postwar period. Works pro and
con are included. Although we are focusing on the
postwar era, most of the literature on this subject
begins in the early 1970´s after the Japanese had made
successful inroads into the world economy.

The material covered here is limited to the
English language, and largely addresses the question of
industrial policy from a U.S. perspective. Books,
short monographs, U.S. government documents, Japanese
government reports, and articles make up the
bibliography´s contents. Only articles that have a
direct bearing on Japan´s industrial policy or its
economic growth have been selected. More latitude was
given to books, since they cover a subject matter in
greater depth, relating it to a wider range of social
and economic relations. Articles from newspapers, news
magazines, and the like have been excluded.

INTRODUCTION

The industrial policy that each government pursues influences that country´s rate of economic growth and its success in meeting social needs. The policy instruments vary according to the history and experience of the nation, but include a widening array of measures, including monetary policy, fiscal controls, and trade restrictions on the one hand, and industrial targeting, government-sponsored research and development, and direct intervention in the economy, on the other.

Since 1945, the balance of economic power among advanced industrial nations has shifted, with Japan´s rapid postwar economic growth. Its competitive position has signalled changes in all the other developed economies, in response to the new Japanese challenge. And less-developed nations have noted the Japanese growth pattern as a model to emulate. In recent decades, Japan´s economy has accomplished remarkable structural readjustments with relatively little friction. These factors have placed Japan at the center of research on industrial policy, because its dramatic success has been in part the result of its strong public and private cooperation in economic planning.

The need to assess Japanese industrial policy has been particularly acute in the United States, where economic growth and productivity have been lagging. Debates in the Congress and private industry have centered on the role of government in the economy, and an understanding of the Japanese experience is seen as the key to developing more successful economic strategies for the U.S.

The Japanese economic "miracle," however, caught the U.S. establishment by surprise, and relatively few studies in English were published about the postwar economic policies of Japan before 1970. Myths about a monolithic government-industry collaboration in Japan began to stereotype the Japanese economy under the rubric of "Japan, Inc.," and there was a paucity of factual information. Once the significance of Japanese economic growth began to register, however, there was a

rush to fill in the research gap. There is now so much
material available that its volume poses an obstacle to
understanding.

The present bibliography seeks to arm the
researcher with a subject guide to works on Japanese
industrial policy and its role in the postwar
performance of the Japanese economy.

The themes which appear in the industrial policy
debates are complex, and many issues are raised in
addition to questions about Japanese industrial policy
per se. First is the explanation of the causes of
Japan's rapid postwar growth. The role of industrial
policy is emphasized by some, while market mechanisms
are cited by others. In some views, the institutional
framework and Japanese culture are chiefly responsible
for the unusual economic growth, with the behavior of
workers and managers seen as peculiar to Japan. Other
writers emphasize the universality of the Japanese
experience, and claim that the rapid economic growth
pattern can be replicated in other nations.

The subjects considered in the present work are
broad enough to provide the whole context for an
understanding of how Japanese industrial policy works,
and how it has influenced economic growth in Japan.
The international ramifications of Japanese industrial
policy are also presented, with particular attention to
U.S.-Japanese relations.

Japan's competitive edge manifests itself in
specific industries, so case studies of industrial
sectors are essential to an assessment of industrial
policy. As international competition varies, industry
by industry, so does industrial policy. In the high
technology fields Japan's success has captured special
attention.

The large-scale research and development efforts
which have given rise to Japan's technological growth
have required the development of an appropriate
financial organization, guided by Japanese industrial
policy. And to permit rapid changes in technology, the
structure of industry and the structure of the firm
itself have developed great flexibility. Industrial
policies have been shaped by the nature of the Japanese
firm, and at the same time, the nature of the firm's
management has been influenced by industrial policies.
The Japanese approach to decision-making by consensus
is a distinguishing feature of the financial and
management patterns considered.

A final viewpoint on the impact of industrial
policy in Japan is one in which the productivity of the
workforce is placed at the base of rapid economic

growth. Studies which investigate the causes of
productivity growth in Japan and delineate the patterns
of relationships between management and workforce are
therefore included.

The significance of the Japanese position in the
world economy is now being recognized. The industrial
policies which are shaping that position have thus
earned new importance. For the future, there are
expectations for more rapid changes, and in many of the
works cited, there are speculations on Japan´s
management of its economy, based on the flexibility it
has shown since the Second World War.

To aid the use of this bibliography, an Authors
and Editors Index, a Title Index, and a Subject Index
have been created. As the Table of Contents shows,
there are eight chapters covering various economic and
social aspects of Japanese industrial policy. An
attempt has been made to place material under the most
appropriate heading, but this is often ambiguous. It
is hoped the Subject Index will help correct this
classification problem, and make these writings more
accessible.

I. JAPANESE INDUSTRIAL POLICY

This chapter covers works directly concerned with Japan´s industrial policies in the postwar period. These works primarily focus on the government-business relationship in the formulation of economic and industrial policy and their effects on economic performance. Writings on particular aspects of the Japanese economy and industrial policy are placed in other chapters.

1. Abegglen, James C., ed. Business Strategies for Japan. Toyko: Sophia University, 1970.

   Written with the idea that Japan´s growth is an epochal development for the world, this book examines the factors that made Japan grow. The handling of human resources, the role of the government, and future prospects are treated. Serving as both a vast market opportunity for other Western economies, Japan also poses a serious competitive threat. Organizational change, financing, the government-business partnership, and competition with the U.S. are described. Strategies for Japan and its economic partners are outlined, including the investment in Japan, the technology potential, marketing in Japan, and recruiting for operations in Japan. Projections of Japan´s growth in the next ten years are offered.

2. Baxter, J. D. "Japan Shifts Its World Trade Sights." Iron Age: The Metalworking Management Newsweekly. 223.44 (Dec. 17, 1980): 36-37.

   This article describes the main features in Japan´s recent shift in its industrial strategies and priorities. Their major effort will concentrate on becoming a leading technological innovator. Evidence is provided to demonstrate the reality of Japan´s strategy shift. Plant and equipment spending for 1960-1979 is given, along with machine tool consumption for the same period.

3. Boltho, Andrea. "Was Japan´s Industrial Policy Successful?" Cambridge Journal of Economics. 9.2 (June 1985): 187-201.

This paper examines the argument that Japan's industrial policy has been relatively less effective than has been claimed. But it is concluded the industrial policy has indeed been far more effective than that of the other major Western economies in the same period. Rebuttals are offered to three criticisms of Japanese industrial policy: that the policy instruments have been too limited in scope to achieve their desired ends, that the policy ideas have been ineffectual, and that the success of the Japanese economy has been the result of other factors besides the industrial policy. In each of these critiques, evidence is offered in support of the industrial policies of Japan. Those policies are credited with having a major influence on the course of the economy in Japan.

4. Boyer, E. "How Japan Manages Declining Industries." _Fortune_. 107.1 (Jan. 10, 1983): 25-30.

The basic characteristics of Japan's policy to manage declining industries are outlined. A description is given of the application of the "Depressed Industries Law" (1978). A basic feature of the policy is joint government-business cooperation in eliminating unwanted factories and machinery. Examples of declined industries are reviewed. Statistics are given for 1977-1982.

5. Bryant, William E. _Japanese Private Economic Diplomacy: An Analysis of Business-Government Linkages_. New York: Praeger Publishers, 1975.

Japan's use of the technique of cooperative business competition is described. While the production of a very favorable business climate has been attributed to a monolithic Japan, Inc., consisting of a conservative business-government elite, there are actually competing interests at work. The underlying interests are identified and examined. The use of economic missions and businessmen as roving ambassadors is studied. International conferences, committees, and other examples of business diplomacy are outlined.

6. Doe, P. "Playing It Cool with Japan Incorporated's Red Hot Education Mama." _Electronic Business_. 9.9 (Aug. 1983): 70,72.

The Japanense Minstry of International Trade and Industry (MITI) is examined in light of the highly publicized efforts it has effected in the area of subsidies to Japanese firms. Its use of cartels and restrictions on imports are also outlined.

From the point of view of the U.S. trade position,
it would be important for Japan to begin to see
its activities in a different context.

7. Drucker, P. F. "Behind Japan's Success." Harvard
   Business Review. 59.1 (Jan./Feb. 1981): 83-90.

   The success of Japan's industrial policy is
   analyzed. Contrary to Western opinion, Japan's
   economy is not an all powerful megalith of a
   business and government partnership. Taking the
   automobile industry as an example, the author
   emphasizes the role of competition. It is however
   secondary to the national interest as formulated
   by Japan's industrial policy. The West focuses
   more on the economic interest of the corporation.
   Additionally, the Japanese upper management spent
   considerably more time on human relations. In
   short, the Japanese have found a way to manage a
   pluralistic society.

8. Freeman, Richard T. "Japan's Adjustment to OPEC
   Increases." Executive. 7.3 (Summer 1981): 47-50.

   Japan has successfully adjusted to oil price
   increases in recent years. Since Japan imports
   all of its oil (constituting a major proportion of
   its energy needs), its result are impressive. The
   readjustment success can be attributed to policy
   measures taken between the two oil crises and the
   institutional organization of the Japanese economy
   which aid in effective allocation of resources.
   Important factors in this adjustment include large
   productivity increases, wage restraint on the part
   of Japanese workers, a decrease in the use of
   imported oil, tax incentives for energy efficient
   equipment, and a highly flexible and effective
   industrial policy.

9. Frenkel, Orit. "Flying High: A Case Study of
   Japanese Industrial Policy." Journal of Policy
   Analysis and Management. 3.3 (Spring 1984): 406-
   20.

   Japan's industrial policy is considered to be
   highly flexible and adaptive, and it involves much
   more than simply identifying preferred industries
   in order to insure their success. The world
   aerospace industry, which Japan has entered even
   though it is handicapped by the lack of a domestic
   market, is a case in point. The means by which
   Japan has begun to alter the structure of the
   market in which it hopes to compete is discussed.

10. Gold, Bela. "Some International Differences in
    Approaches to Industrial Policy." Contemporary

Policy Issues. 4.1 (Jan. 1986): 12-22.

Various different outlooks on the industrial
policy debate are examined. Past experiences in
industrial policy are considered, differences
among various countries´ approaches are traced,
and the main features of a policy that tends to
enhance the competitive position of the country
itself are described. Some conclusions are
derived from studies of various countries. For
example, policy should attempt to strengthen the
growth of new technology and help to reduce the
burdens of research and risk-taking which are
connected with high-tech industry. A partnership
of government and industry is advocated.

11. Hadley, Eleanor M. "The Secret of Japan´s
    Success." Challenge. 26.2 (May/June 1983): 4-10.

    Japan´s industrial policy is an underlying reason
    why it competes so well internationally. This
    provides a high degree of cooperation between the
    government and private industry. By assuming a
    portion of the risk, the government allows
    companies, and industries as a whole, to be more
    adventurous in their product development and
    market strategies. Further the government
    promotes productivity by the creation of tax
    benefits to companies performing efficiently. The
    automobile and computer industries have
    particularly benefited from government support.
    U.S. economic policy is based totally on market
    forces, and hence American companies do not enjoy
    the support their Japanese counterparts do. U.S.
    capital is furthermore free to seek profits in any
    nation, regardless of its effects on the domestic
    economy.

12. Hagen, Everett E., ed. Planning Economic
    Development. Homewood Ill.: Richard D. Irwin,
    Inc., 1963.

    This book examines the economic planning policies
    of nine countries, including Japan. Themes that
    are common to all include the impact of government
    on the economic system, national goals, and
    definitions of economic planning itself. Japan is
    distinguished by the speed of its economic growth
    and the formal nature of its economic planning.
    Historical origins are traced, and postwar
    objectives and procedures are outlined.

13. Hickman, Bert G., ed. Quantitative Planning of
    Economic Policy. A Conference of the Social
    Science Research Council Committee on Economic
    Stability. Washington, D.C.: Brookings

Institution, 1965.

Papers presented are from an international
conference held at the Brookings Institution
August 19-24, 1963. Leading developments in the
field of quantitative policy planning and research
in France, Japan, and the Netherlands were
analyzed. Topics develop the themes of economic
policy theory, policy models and applications,
effectiveness of planning techniques, and research
suggestions. Eleven chapters are presented, with
empirical and theoretical implications.

14. Horvath, Dezso, and Charles McMillan. "Industrial
Planning in Japan." California Management Review.
23.1 (Fall 1980): 11-21.

Seeing the essence of the "Japan, Inc." operation
as a set of channels for economic decision making
among well-informed actors, this study focuses on
the process of industrial planning. The economic
planning of Japan is described, both in its use of
stabilization policy and the setting of industrial
structure goals. Industry sectors are viewed in
terms of portfolio approach. Export strategy and
foreign investment are investigated.

15. Hyoe, Murakami, and Johannes Hirschmeier, eds.
Politics and Ecomomics in Contemporary Japan.
Tokyo: Japan Culture Institute, 1979.

The political economy of Japan presumes that the
public realms of politics and economics cooperate
toward a common goal to which the individual is
subordinated. This book aims to show how this
inter-relationship between the individual, the
group to which he belongs, and the state operates
and how differences in the political economies of
Japan and the West can be seen to arise from
different cultural backgrounds. Divided into two
parts, the first concentrates on Japanese
politics, while the second focuses on its
economics. In this second part, the myth and
reality of "Japan, Inc." is examined, as well as
labor unions, small business, agriculture,
bankruptcy, and what lies behind the "Made in
Japan" label.

16. Ichimura, Shinichi. Japanese Industrial
Restructuring Policies, 1945-1979. Discussion
Paper 106. Kyoto, Japan: Center for Southeast
Asian Studies, Kyoto University, 1979.

A brief overview of Japan's industrial
restructuring policies for the 1945-1979 period is
provided in this monograph. It sketches the

principal economic features of the period and the
government-business relations that enabled the
Japanese economy to grow and successfully to
compete in international markets. Policies toward
high-tech, automobile, and other industries are
discussed.

17. Ike, Nobutaka. Japanese Politics: Patron-Client
    Democracy. 2nd ed. New York: Knopf, 1972.

    As a behaviorially based view of the Japanese
    political system, this book offers a description
    of the social system as one which differs
    fundamentally from systems in the West. There are
    treatments of the setting, the political forces,
    the process, and the current status of Japanese
    politics. There is a review of the last ten
    years´ scholarship in a compact form.

18. Industrial Structure Council. The Vision of MITI
    Policies in 1980s: Summary. Tokyo: MITI
    Information Office, 1980.

    This short monograph projects likely policies that
    the Ministry of International Trade and Industry
    will formulate in the 1980´s. It outlines trends
    in international markets and competition, and sees
    Japan´s future lying in the continued development
    of its high-tech industries and in developing
    basic technology research.

19. Japan. Economic Planning Agency. Basic Economic
    and Social Plan 1973-1977: Toward a Vigorous
    Welfare Society. Tokyo: Printing Office, Ministry
    of Finance, 1973.

    Indicative planning guidelines are given for
    economic policy objectives in Japan. An
    explanation is provided for the need to update and
    revise the 1970´s plan. Goals of the present plan
    are detailed with a profile of the Japanese
    economy in 1977. Major issues include economic
    growth, environment, land use and infrastructure,
    and welfare. Investments by sector are outlined.
    Discussions and reviews are also given for pricing
    policy, foreign trade policy, industrial and
    scientific policies, fiscal and monetary policies,
    and growth, savings, investments, and incomes
    policy.

20. Japan. Economic Planning Agency. New Economic and
    Social Development Plan, 1970-1975. Tokyo?:
    Economic Planning Agency, 1970.

    This official Japanese plan emphasizes as major
    goals the stabilization of prices, coping with

internationalization and liberalized trade, and
renovating the structure of industry. Specific
goals are identified. There are problems with
sectors that are having difficulty competing.
Small business productivity needs attention.
Issues for long-term well-being such as the
environment are also addressed. Means of reaching
goals included capitalization, educational
development, fiscal policies, and administration.
Prospects for the future are discussed.

21. Japan. Economic Planning Agency. New Economic and
    Social Seven-Year Plan. Tokyo: Economic Planning
    Agency, 1979.

    This official economic plan identifies the major
    goals for the economy. Trade, prices, and
    different sectors with special problems are
    considered. The means by which the goals will be
    reached are discussed. Administrative and fiscal
    policies are also identified.

22. Japan. Economic Planning Agency. New Long Range
    Economic Plan of Japan, 1961-1970: Doubling
    National Income Plan. Tokyo: Economic Planning
    Agency, 1961.

    Goals to be targeted for the economic growth of
    Japan are outlined in this official government
    paper. Production, trade, and special sectors are
    treated. The means by which government policy
    will help to attain goals are given.

23. Japan. Ministry of International Trade and
    Industry. Background Information on Japan's
    Industrial Policy. Tokyo: MITI, 1983.

    The basic features of the Japanese economy and the
    functions of its industrial policy are described.
    This report examines the role of private firms and
    managerial efforts in their competition with other
    Western countries. It covers subsidies and
    regulations in the government's guidance of the
    economy and Japan's conformation to the GATT trade
    agreements. Criticism is made of industrial
    policy as a target policy. The industrial policy
    of the U.S. is reviewed in the context of
    approaches to the promotion of high-tech
    industries. Recommendations are made for
    adjustment of the Japanese industrial policy.

24. Japan. Ministry of International Trade and
    Industry. Features of the Industrial Policy of
    Japan. Tokyo: MITI, 1983.

    The philosophy behind Japan's industrial policy is

presented along with the objectives of the current
industrial policy. It discusses the areas of
major concern and reviews the planning process and
methods of consensus and implication. An outline
is given of the challenges and the outlook for the
1980´s.

25. Japan. Ministry of International Trade and
    Industry. The Industrial Structure of Japan in
    the 1980s: Summary: Future Outlook and Tasks.
    Background Information 44. Tokyo: MITI, 1981.

    A popular presentation of Japan´s industrial
    structure, its outlook and objectives in the
    1980´s. It states the policy options for energy
    consumption, technological innovations, plant and
    equipment investment in the private sector,
    allocation of labor, and the expansion of the
    service sector. Statistics provided for 1955-
    1980.

26. Japan. Ministry of International Trade and
    Industry. Japanese Industrial Policy. Japan
    Reporting 4. Tokyo: MITI, 1981.

    This report outlines the Japan´s economic
    development and industrial policies in the postwar
    period, covering various aspects of its industrial
    policy. It describes basic philosophy behind its
    industrial policy, the degree of the government´s
    intervention, and the policy instruments employed.
    Major factors contributing to the development of
    the Japanese economy are presented, as well as the
    tasks and perspectives for the 1980´s.

27. Japan. Ministry of International Trade and
    Industry. Japan´s Industrial Structure: A Long
    Range Vision. 2 vols. Tokyo: Japan External
    Trade Organization [sold by Press International],
    1975.

    The promotion of industrial restructuring through
    various policy measures is discussed. There is
    attention given to the outlook for the nation as a
    whole, its needs and resources. Prospects for the
    major industries are reviewed, and particular
    consideration is given to the small business
    sector´s special needs. Regional differences are
    outlined, and the future of internationalization
    is projected. Energy resources and the future of
    energy needs in Japan is taken up, and the future
    for technological development is also considered.

28. Japan Economic Research Center. Economic Planning
    and Macroeconomic Policy: Papers and Proceedings
    of a Conference Held by The Japan Economic

Research Center in September, 1970. 2 vols.
Tokyo: Japan Economic Research Center, 1971.

The Conference's aim was to provide a
retrospective overview of the role of economic
planning in the policy making and direction of
postwar Japan. Topics include the characteristics
of planning, the machinery for implementation of
policy, the quantitative and regional aspects of
planning, the social aspects of planning and the
international viewpoint. The political situation
is also discussed.

29. Johnson, Chalmers A. "The Institutional
    Foundations of Japanese Industrial Policy."
    California Management Review. 27.4 (Summer
    1985): 59-69.

    The relationship between Japan's industries and
    governmental agencies is analyzed, with attention
    to the theoretical and the political aspects of
    the subject. The success of Japanese industries
    in recent years is the result, at least in part,
    of the activities of the Ministry for Inter-
    national Trade and Industry, which has been
    setting the policy. Among the most important
    policies are these: the allocation of capital to
    certain preferred industries, the identification
    of growth goals for special industries, and the
    arrangement of ways to support declining sectors
    of the economy. Some conclusions are drawn in
    respect of the position of Japan's competitors.
    From their point of view it would be wise to
    undertake to understand the Japanese experience.

30. Johnson, Chalmers A. Japan's Public Policy
    Companies. American Enterprise Institute - Hoover
    Policy Studies 24; Hoover Institution Studies 60.
    Washington, D.C.: American Enterprise Institute
    for Public Policy Research, 1978.

    An analysis is given of the significance of
    Japanese public corporations and of the mixed
    public-private enterprises. It describes the
    government-business relationship as well as the
    government's role in economic and industrial
    policymaking, contrasting it with the West. Types
    and origins of public companies are presented
    along with a detailing of their financing and
    control. The energy sector in particular is
    examined. And lastly, the relationship between
    public corporations and bureaucratism is drawn.

31. Johnson, Chalmers A. MITI and the Japanese
    Miracle: The Growth of Industrial Policy, 1925-
    1975. Stanford, Calif.: Stanford University

Press, 1982.

This book highlights the historical role of the
Japanese government in providing guidance for
economic growth and development. The Japanese
government-business relation is characterized as a
"developmental or plan-rational" state, while the
U.S. is considered a "regulatory" state and the
Soviet Union as "plan-ideological" and "command"
state. It investigates the history of the
Ministry of International Trade and Industry with
a detailed study of MITI´s predecessors and the
role they played in the development of the
Japanese economy. The continuity of government
guidance in the growth of Japan´s economy is
stressed with particular emphasis on MITI´s role
in the postwar period. The dominant feature of
the Japanese state is the setting of substantial
social and economic goals. Economic growth is
achieved through strong, but indirect, guidance
mechanisms rather than outright control and
ownership of plants and factories.

32. Kaplan, Eugene J. Japan: The Government-Business
    Relationship: A Guide for the American
    Businessman. Washington, D.C.: U.S. Bureau of
    International Commerce, 1972.

    This study investigates the extent, methods, and
    effectiveness of government-business relations in
    Japan. It begins with an overview of Japan´s
    rapid economic growth in the 1960´s and its impact
    on the U.S. Next a model of Japanese business-
    government relationship is developed, sketching
    its general workings. A description is given of
    the reasons behind government and business
    interaction and the mechanisms by which agreement
    is reached on national economic goals and targets
    and the methods of implementation. This model in
    turn is tested against the findings of specific
    studies of government-business interaction in
    three major Japanese high growth industries -
    computers, automobiles, and steel.

33. Komiya, Ryutaro. "Economic Planning in Japan."
    Challenge. 18.2 (May/June 1975): 9-20.

    The activities of the Japanese industrial policy-
    makers have recently been confined to such things
    as forecasting at the industry level and less
    attention has been given to the making of
    decisions that really control the economy. The
    control of pollution, and the safeguarding of the
    rights of the consumer are also often discussed.
    Other issues include the maintenance of good
    relations with other countries and the

stabilizing of pricing on the international markets.

34. Kraar, Louis. "Adversity is Helping the Japanese Refashion Their Future." Fortune. 94.4 (Oct. 1976): 126-131, 202, 206.

A popular account of Japan's need to restructure its economy and politics. The Economic Planning Agency and MITI seek a new policy for promoting knowledge-intensive industries. Greater emphasis will be placed on a corporation's own ingenuity for future growth. Policies are aimed at eliminating wasteful habits, increasing efficiency, and cutting costs.

35. Kurihara, Kenneth K. "Observations on Japan's Ten-Year Growth Plan." Kyklos. 15 (1962): 787-799.

This paper analyzes the Japanese government's economic plans for 1961-70. The differences from plans of other nations are noted, and the need for the balance of effective demand and the growth of productive capacity is described. Technological innovations and growth potential are investigated, and the investment-consumption relation is examined. Public policy and growth is analyzed.

36. Magaziner, Ira C., and Thomas M. Hout. Japanese Industrial Policy. Policy Papers in Iinternational Affairs 15. Berkeley: Institute of International Studies, University of California, 1980.

This book analyzes Japan's industrial policy in terms of the basic competitive and economic forces which exist within all businesses. The application of government resources and influence to industrial affairs must be studied with a thorough understanding of how competition varies by industry and over time. National priorities and fast growth markets are important factors in determining industrial policy, but it is also important to recognize that industrial policy is an integral part of the international competitive system. Thus the context for industrial policy in Japan is described, and the people who make policy are identified. Case studies of policy in particular industries are also offered.

37. McIntyre, W. "Japanese Industry Becomes One Great Rethink Tank." Japan. 63 (Sept. 1977): 22-34.

The international oil crisis is causing changes in Japan's growth policy. Rethinking of industrial

policy is occurring on many issues: the role of
the government, energy sources and its effect on
industrial structure, foreign trade, and
international competition. A major consequence of
the recession is the restructuring of various
industries, in particular, a move away from
energy-intensive to high-tech ones. Alternative
plans are discussed and the effects on employment.

38. Miyazaki, Isamu. "Economic Planning in Postwar
Japan." The Developing Economies. 8.4 (Dec.
1970): 369-385.

This article explores the mechanisms by which
Japanese economic plans have been introduced and
followed by the public and private sectors.
Nearly a dozen such plans have been adopted, as
indicative and not imperative promulgations.
Private sector compliance has been sought and
usually gained, and public intervention has been
avoided except in the case of declining industries
and some infant industries. The share of
government activities in the economy has
increased, as a means of promoting social welfare,
education, and the like. A major objective of an
economic plan is to clarify the measures which the
government will take in achieving the target of
its policy, such as the increase in social
overhead capital, an expansion in education,
promotion of social security, and appropriate
demand management. Its targets are simply
forecasts, though some restrictions are set up.
Forecasts were generally not accurate in early
plans, and growth is now being moderated in recent
plans.

39. Nakagawa, Keiichiro, ed. Government and Business:
Proceedings of the Fifth Fuji Conference.
International Conference on Business History, 5th,
Fuji Education Center, 1978. Tokyo: University of
Tokyo Press, 1980.

From a business history perspective, the
conference reports offer studies on business-
government relations in England, Germany, the
United States, and Japan. For Japan, the stages
of industrialization are traced, from pre-
conditions, to take-off, and then maturation. The
sociology of the state and the individual is
needed to understand the topic fully. Discussions
of each paper are given.

40. Nakagawa, Yatsuhiro, and Nobumasa Ota. The
Japanese-Style Economic System: A New Balance
Between Intervention and Freedom. Reference
Reading Series 4. Tokyo: Foreign Press Centre,

1981.

This short monograph gives an overview of Japan's
industrial policy and the government-business
relations which have allowed the Japanese economy
and international trade to be so successful. This
has been done in the context of a competitive
domestic market and the government's involvement
in capital markets and in restricting foreign
access to Japanese markets. Greater freedom is
seen to be developing in these areas.

41. Organisation for Economic Cooperation and
    Development. The Aims and Instruments of
    Industrial Policy: A Comparative Study. Paris:
    OECD, 1975.

    This book clarifies the concept of industrial
    policy by analyzing the policies of OECD
    countries. Special subject areas, such as
    regional development, multi-national enterprises,
    management education, and small and medium-sized
    businesses are introduced. Industrial policy has
    a set of objectives and a framework, and has an
    impact on industrial climate. Promotion of
    expansion, innovation and efficiency is discussed.
    Policy for specific sectors is examined, along
    with export and competition promotion. Social
    aspects of policy are described. Conclusions are
    offered regarding international aspects.

42. Organisation for Economic Cooperation and
    Development. The Industrial Policy of Japan.
    Paris: OECD, 1972.

    This report provides material on policy
    instruments and issues as seen from the government
    angle. Many countries are interested in Japanese
    success formulas, though not all the elements in
    the Japanese policy mix are relevant to other
    nations, as some depend on psychological factors,
    history, tradition and geographic features of
    Japan. Topics include the geography, the
    administrative framework and the main policy
    instruments of Japan. Attention is also given to
    structural change, small business, technological
    stimulation, manpower, foreign trade, cooperation
    with the developing countries, capital
    liberalization, and consumer and environmental
    protection.

43. Panhuyzen, W. van den. "Japan's Industrial
    Policy: From Promotion to Protection."
    Tijdschrift voor Economie en Management. 30.1
    (1985): 45-74.

This article describes how Japan´s agressive
industrial policy, as it was implemented until the
mid 1970s, was facilitated by structural
characteristics of the Japanese economy, apart
from cheap labour and capital. However from the
mid 1970s, Japan´s industrial policy shifted from
reaching out for world markets to the internal
problems of depressed industries with excessive
production capacity. Information is provided on
Japan´s financial structure, organization and
decision making, the country´s research and
development programs, and its industrial policy.

44. Pugel, T. A. "Japan´s Industrial Policy:
Instruments, Trends, and Effects." Journal of
Comparative Economics. 8.4 (Dec. 1984): 420-435.

Japan´s government policies have promoted
industrial growth in various ways since 1945.
Planning, investment rates, capital development,
and high productivity have been elements of the
success of Japan´s economy. For the first twenty
years it was manufacturing in basic industries
that received the most attention. Then high tech
became the featured area. Tax policies have
contributed significantly to Japan´s growth.

45. Rapp, William V. "Japan: Its Industrial Policies
and Corporate Behavior." Columbia Journal of
World Business. 12.1 (Spring 1977): 38-48.

The reasons why the Japanese economy has fared
well during periods of recession are explored.
Though some economists had predicted that the
structure of Japan´s labor relations would make it
difficult for the economy to withstand pressure,
it appears that the industrial supply structure is
responsible for Japan´s demonstrated success in
hard times. Japan has, for example, high levels
of very up to date and productive firms engaged in
manufacture of basic materials that consistently
show relatively strong demand worldwide.

46. Ruangskul, N. "The Forward Looking Japanese."
Thailand Business. 4.12 (Oct. 1981): 35-37.

A look is taken at the Japanese industrial policy
for the 1980´s. Priorities of their economic plan
include the export-oriented industries, the
allocation of labor, and small and medium sized
industries.

47. Sakoh, Katsuro, and Philip H. Trezise. "Japanese
Economic Success: Industrial Policy or Free
Market?." Cato Journal. 4.2 (Fall 1984): 521-
548.

Japan's post World War II economic growth is
examined in the light of four basic questions: 1)
What was the role of the Japanese government in
the period of economic expansion? 2) What was the
extent of targeting industries, and were they
successful? 3) To what extent was private
investment the result of business-government
coordination? and 4) What role did the market play
in this period? From a study of this period, the
author answers 1) the role of the state in the
economy was minimal; 2) high-growth industries
were not targeted; 3) financing was generated
primarily from private sources; and 4) key
investment decisions were made by corporate
executives. The government aided this economic
success by maintaining a small and balanced
budget, low and stable interest rates, low tax
rates, and stable prices. By so doing, the
government provided a favorable economic
environment for growth to occur. The
microeconomic role of the Japanese state is
overstated in this period, where its restraints
were more important than its interventions.

48. Sawada, J. "Government Industrial Policy for a
    Healthy World Economy." Technological Forecasting
    & Social Change. 24.2 (Oct. 1983): 95-105.

    The industrial policies of Japan are examined,
    with a focus on the Ministry of International
    Trade and Industry. The use of both market
    mechanisms and restructuring of industry are
    traced for the past twenty-five years.

49. Saxonhouse, Gary R. "What Is All This About
    `Industrial Targeting´ in Japan?" World Economy.
    6.3 (Sept. 1983): 253-273.

    It is the general perception that the Japanese
    government provides a great deal of support to the
    rapid growing high-technology industries, enabling
    them to dominate foreign markets. The government
    strategy includes tariff protection, direct
    subsidies, and preferred credit terms. Actually,
    the Japanese government provides less formal aid
    to high-tech industries than most other economies.
    Japan's government intervention revolves around
    replacing the market for the allocation of
    capital, including research and development
    projects. In other industrial economies this is
    achieved as the by-product of well-functioning
    markets. Japan's informal industrial policy is
    essentially result of its financial system.

50. Sekiguchi, Sueo, and Toshihiro Horiuchi. "Myth
    and Reality of Japan's Industrial Policies."

World Economy. 8.4 (Dec. 1985): 373-391.

Some of the characteristics of Japanese industrial
policy are outlined. Among the most important
ones appears the tendency for Japan to use
tariffs, import quotas, subsidies, and other means
of regulation for the purpose of protecting
nascent industries. When industries are new, it
is argued that this protection is necessary
because of the difficulties and risks inherent in
the development of a new product. There is a
review of laws that enabled the Japanese
government to control developing industrial
sectors, with attention given to the state of the
legislation in 1945, 1978 and 1983. Some
discussion of the controversies which arise from
the interference with the free market by the
Japanese government is provided. A statistical
overview of government subsidies to private R&D
activities by types is given for 1957-80, as well
as the adjustment process of designated industries
under the Act for Specified Depressed Industries,
1977-1981.

51. Shimokobe, Atsushi. "Concepts and Methodology of
    Regional Development." The Developing Economies.
    8.4 (Dec. 1970): 497-511.

    Regional development in Japan is examined in the
    1950's during the recovery period and during the
    1960's when growth was extraordinarily high. An
    explanation of the comprehensive national
    development plan of 1969 is offered. Problems of
    regional development are discussed as related to
    recent environmental changes.

52. Shinohara, Miyohei. "MITI'S Industrial Policy and
    Japanese Industrial Organization: A Retrospective
    Evaluation." The Developing Economies. 14.4
    (December 1976): 366-380.

    Diverging views of the MITI in Japan have been
    offered, in which the agency is decried as the
    monolithic source of big business conglomeration.
    This view is considered in terms of the acutal
    structure of business groups in Japan. General
    trading companies and large-scale mergers are
    delineated. Policies which tend to favor the
    development of "infant" industries are examined.
    While the MITI policies are almost universally
    considered to run counter to the nation's anti-
    monopoly laws, this article advocates their
    assessment in a larger perspective, since the MITI
    policies are so important for the success of the
    present economy.

53. Storella, M. C. "Japan's Industrial Policy: A
    Foreigner's View." Tokyo Financial Review. 8.10
    (Oct. 1983): 1-5.

    A general analysis of the nature of Japan's
    industrial policy is given with its effects and
    its applicability for other nations. Statistics
    are provided for 1965-81.

54. Struthers, J. E. "Why Can't We Do What Japan
    Does?." Canadian Business Review. 8.2 (Summer
    1981): 24-26.

    A number of factors contribute to Japan's success
    in production and exports: 1) its industrial
    policy creates a coordinated effort between
    government, business, and labor; 2) its plants are
    relatively new; 3) the lifetime employment
    attitudes of its workers; 4) its low defense
    expenditures permit greater capital investments
    possible; 5) high-tech tools of production, for
    example robots, increase quality at lower cost;
    and 6) its traditional cultural austerity enhances
    the general production effort. Japan's economic
    recovery since the war has been created by special
    circumstances which would be difficult to
    transplant to the West.

55. Trezise, Philip H. "Industrial Policy Is Not the
    Major Reason for Japan's Success." Brookings
    Review. 1.3 (Spring 1983): 13-18.

    The Japanese government has contributed
    significantly to Japanese growth, but it has not
    been responsible to a decisive degree for the
    economic success of Japanese industry. Decision-
    making at the level of microeconomics has been
    influenced by agencies such as the Economic
    Planning Agency, the Ministry of International
    Trade and Industry, and the Fiscal Loan and
    Investment Program, but this does not mean the
    economy is not at the same time running as a free-
    market economy. There are many different interest
    groups and levels of productivity within the
    system, and resources are allocated according to
    market principles of supply and demand.
    Government budgets are planned in a democratic
    manner, and the decisions regarding capital
    formation are in the hands of the individual
    capitalists. Thus the overall control of the
    economy cannot be said to rest with the industrial
    policy which is articulated by the government.

56. Tsuruta, Toshimasa. "The Myth of Japan Inc."
    Technology Review. 86.5 (July 1983): 42-48.

It has been widely asserted that Japanese economic
growth has been the result of a strongly
government controlled industrial policy. Some
writers have referred to the Japanese government-
industry partnership as "Japan Inc." since 1970.
But this paper contests the assumption that the
Japanese government has intervened excessively in
the economic sphere, in particular, in the
domestic markets within Japan. Many factors
prevented the Japanese government from dominating
the economy, such as the democratic forces in its
parliamentary structure, and the market
competition in its economic structure. In many
cases, the domestic market in Japan acted as a
stimulant to its industry, and the success of
Japanese products on the international market was
the result of this highly innovative spirit in the
domestic marketplace. Japanese industrial policy
can be seen to have experienced a historical
development, and since the war it has gone through
several distinct phases. Most of the development
can be accounted for in terms of the responses to
individual problems, as they arose. And the
belief that Japan's government had a monolithic
plan which dictated economic growth is in part the
result of the Ministry of International Trade and
Industry (MITI). This agency, however, it can be
concluded, did not exert such strong controls as
it has been thought, especially in the areas of
domestic trade and exports.

57. Ueno, H. "Conception and Evaluation of Japanese
    Industrial Policy." Japanese Economic Studies.
    75.2 (Winter 1976/77): 1-61.

    This discussion on postwar Japanese industrial
    policy is concerned with the consequences of land
    and resource limitations, the role of the
    international division of labor, and the effect of
    industrial policy via direct government
    interventions. An estimate of the role of the
    selective allocation of funds and protective
    policies favoring certain sectors is given. The
    Japanese mass production system and consequences
    of its industrial policy are considered.

58. United States. Congress. Joint Economic Committee.
    Industrial Policy: Japan's Flexible Approach:
    Report to the Chairman, Joint Economic Committee
    United States Congress by the Comptroller General
    of the United States.. Washington, D.C.: U.S.
    General Accounting Office, 1982.

    This report is a review of the Japanese industrial
    policy. Chief elements are analyzed and the
    ability of the various policy measures to be used

in changing circumstances is investigated. The
role of industrial policy in the creation of a
successful economic growth record is assessed.
Some implications for U.S. are offered.

59. United States. Congress. Joint Economic Committee.
    Japanese Industrial and Labor Policy: Hearing
    before the Joint Economic Committee, Congress of
    the United States, Ninety-Seventh Congress, Second
    Session, June 23, 1982. Washington, D.C.: G.P.O.,
    1982.

    A report from the Comptroller General of the U.S.
    General Accounting Office is offered regarding
    Japanese industrial policy. The goals of policy
    since the war are described. Measures used by the
    policy are outlined, and policy toward expanding
    and declining industries is examined. The
    flexibility of Japan's policies is pointed out,
    and the success of the policies in meeting
    changing times is investigated. The use of
    industrial policy in the computer, aircraft,
    robotics, shipbuilding and textile industries is
    described.

60. United States. General Accounting Office.
    Industrial Policy: Case Studies in the Japanese
    Experience. Washington D.C.: U.S. General
    Accounting Office, 1982.

    This report uses a case study approach from
    various segments of the Japanese economy to
    investigate the industrial policy employed by
    Japan. The lessons that can be drawn for American
    economic planning are outlined.

61. Wheeler, Jimmy W. Japanese Industrial Development
    Policies in the 1980s: Implications for U.S. Trade
    and Investment: Final Report. Croton-on-Hudson,
    N.Y.: Hudson Institute, 1982.

    This is a report on the policies of Japan
    regarding industrial development. The roles of
    government and the private sector are discussed in
    relation to policy goals. The implications of
    Japanese policy on U.S. trade with Japan are
    considered. U.S. investment in Japan is also
    treated.

62. Yamamura, Kozo. Economic Policy in Postwar Japan:
    Growth Versus Economic Democracy. Berkeley:
    University of California Press, 1967.

    The two major policies in postwar Japan's economic
    leadership were the economic democratization plans
    of the Occupation and the Japanese government's

policy of economic growth. The causes and the
means by which the economic growth policy became
dominant are examined. Market structure is
explored with the issue of technological
efficiency and competition. The Anti-Monopoly Act
is discussed, from its idealistic beginnings to
its eventual erosion. And the concentration of
economic power in general is explained. Other
issues include policy rationales and their effect
on the size and distribution of firms, the
"Zaibatsu" question, and the tax policies. The
impact of policies on labor and wages is
estimated. Conclusions are offered, which make
criticisms of the postwar policies of Japan.

63. Yamanaka, Sadanori. "Japanese Industrial Policy."
    Focus Japan. 10.5 (May 1983): 1-7.

    The basic thinking involved in the industrial
    policy of Japan is explained, with attention to
    the role of the government. Some of the important
    issues for industrial policy debates today are
    outlined, with the international implications they
    bring with them. Various policies of advanced
    economies are described for fostering high tech
    industries and competing in the world economy.

64. Yoshitake, Kiyohiko. An Introduction to Public
    Enterprise in Japan. Beverly Hills, Calif.: Sage
    Publications, 1973.

    Attention is given to a definition of "public
    enterprises," in terms of size and classificatory
    characteristics of significance. A treatment of
    the history of the public enterprise is offered.
    Investment and financing traits are explored, as
    well as the typical industrial relations patterns.
    Governance, control and accountability are also
    discussed.

II. JAPAN´S ECONOMIC DEVELOPMENT

In this chapter works concentrating on Japan´s economic growth and development are included. Industrial policy is considered an integral factor in the economic history of Japan, influencing its capital formation, industrial restructuring, and economic readjustments. General historical analyses of Japan´s rapid economic growth are also considered here.

65. Allen, George C. The Japanese Economy. New York: St. Martin´s Press, 1982.

   In this general overview of the Japanese economy, there is a concentration on the conditions contributing to economic growth and prosperity in the postwar era. The financial system, agriculture, industrial structure and organization, technology, management, and investment are reviewed. The government sector is also described, and the reasons why it has been able to function very effectively in spite of its small relative size are explained. Prewar conditions are traced, the reconstruction is described, and the role of government is analyzed. Finance and management are discussed in turn. Industrial organization and the role of labor is delineated, and foreign trade is outlined, with conclusions as to the achievements of the Japanese system.

66. Allen, George C. Japan´s Economic Expansion. London: Oxford University Press, 1965.

   This book develops the analysis offered in the earlier book about the postwar recovery which Allen published in 1958, concentrating on the changes since 1958. Aspects of the Japanese economy which are profiled include the course of recovery and expansion, growth planning activities, and the role of the financial system. Agriculture, industries such as textile, engineering, steel, chemicals, and energy and the industrial organization of Japan are then examined. Labor and foreign trade are also outlined.

21

67. Allen, George C. <u>Japan´s Economic Policy</u>. New
    York, London: Holmes & Meier, Macmillan, 1980.

    Representing a collection of previously published
    articles, this book traces the author´s interest
    in various areas of the Japanese economic scene.
    At first interest in the financial organization
    and policy is apparent. Then a study of the
    industrial organization appears, and a study of
    the role of the Japanese as exporters of a number
    of manufactures follows. The question of how the
    Japanese have managed to sustain such a rapid
    growth then is taken up, and the role of the
    government, which seems unmistakably large, is
    evaluated. The interplay of government decision-
    making and private initiatives is a theme that
    follows throughout the book.

68. Allen, George C. <u>Japan´s Economic Recovery</u>.
    London: Oxford University Press, 1958.

    Written a short time after the end of the War,
    this book attempts to assess the changes that have
    taken place in Japan in its aftermath. The
    differences which stand out in the economic
    structure of the nation compared with the
    structure it had in the middle 30´s are quite
    significant, and short-term causes are identified.
    A treatment of the agricultural, industrial,
    financial, and labor sectors of the economy
    reveals the strong impact of the United States
    occupation period. Consideration is given to many
    measurable indicators of economic status, such as
    the volume of trade, the size distributions of
    firms, the changes in markets and sources of
    imports, the wholesale price index, the level of
    wages, and other such factors.

69. Allen, George C. <u>A Short Economic History of</u>
    <u>Modern Japan</u>. 4th ed. New York: St. Martin´s
    Press, 1981.

    The first section of the book outlines the
    development of Japanese economics before 1937,
    when war with China began. Industrial and
    financial development and economic policy are
    emphasized. Research into Japanese economic
    history is then extended to cover the period up
    until 1962. In the third edition, some results of
    recent research appear, bringing the book up to
    date as of 1972. The current edition, in 1981,
    has a completely rewritten chapter which treates
    the period 1945-70. As statistics are brought up
    to date, controversies which have arisen as a
    result of an attempt to quantify the historical
    exegesis are aired.

70. Austin, Lewis, ed. <u>Japan: The Paradox of Progress</u>.
New Haven: Yale University Press, 1976.

Japan is at the cutting edge of a worldwide
process of social adaptation, and its potential is
great. With liberal, humanist assumptions, these
writers explore the political variables that
affect Japanese change. Economic factors such as
the land, labor, and capital, as well as
structures of trade, technology and investment are
analyzed. What people in Japan want for their
future is examined.

71. Bieda, Ken. <u>The Structure and Operation of the
Japanese Economy</u>. Sydney: John Wiley and Sons
Australasia, 1970.

This book presents an analysis of Japan's high
rate of economic growth in the postwar period.
During this time the Japanese government has drawn
up economic plans approximately every three years.
It is argued that the role of the government in
ecomomic life cannot be understood apart from the
fact that Japanese society respects advice given
by the government, that government plan's form the
basis of the private sector's own plans, and that
the implementation of these plans is carried out
through fiscal and monetary policies peculiar to
Japan with independent control by various
government institutions. A detailed study is also
given of the Japanese tax system, the agricultural
situation and farmland reform, capital market, the
keiretsu, and the influence of Japan's unique
monetary and industrial structures on economic
growth.

72. Boltho, Andrea. <u>Japan: An Economic Survey, 1953-
1973</u>. London: Oxford University Press, 1975.

Divided into two parts, this book first provides a
summary of Japan's economic development,
structure, and performance since WW II. Starting
with Japan's growth record and cyclical
fluctuations, it proceeds to describe selected
features of the Japanese industrial structure,
particularly its economic dualism and employment
practices. Part II analyzes the factors
contributing to Japan's rapid economic growth.
Attention is focused on capital formation, labor
supply, and the role of government policies and
intervention. In addition, foreign trade and
income distribution are discussed because of their
influence on economic growth. While Japan's
economy is the center of attention, it is placed
in its international context. Implications for
the future are drawn.

73. Cohen, Jerome B. Japan's Postwar Economy.
    Bloomington: Indiana University Press, 1958.

    The nature of Japan's postwar economic recovery is
    presented, while analyzing the factors responsible
    for it. It places Japan's recovery in its
    international context, looks at its people and
    food, and details the relationship between income,
    output, and employment. The changing industrial
    structure is discussed from an historical
    perspective, as well as foreign trade and
    payments. Japan's foreign economic relations are
    covered, particularly with the U.S., Southeast
    Asia, and the Communist Bloc. Also analyzed are
    the economic problems now (1958) confronting
    Japan.

74. Crowley, James B., ed. Modern East Asia: Essays in
    Interpretation. New York: Harcourt, Brace &
    World, Inc., 1970.

    Written toward the aim of enlightening Western
    policy in Asia, this book is dedicated to the
    reduction of fear and conflicts which arise from
    lack of understanding. Historical essays on China
    and Japan are given, with one chapter with five
    essays devoted to the postwar development of the
    Japanese economy. Those topics include the
    occupation, the reconstruction, political economy
    and welfare, future prospects, and readings
    recommendations.

75. Dahlby, T., et al. "Industrial Japan '79." Far
    Eastern Economic Review. 106.50 (Dec. 14, 1979):
    45-63.

    An overview is given of the development and
    structure of Japanese industry. The role of
    technology and industrial policy are major factors
    in the growth of Japan's economy. Case studies
    are presented for some electronics firms.
    Analysis of other industries are explored,
    including their grow prospects. Statistics
    provided for 1965-1985.

76. Denison, Edward F., and William K. Chung. How
    Japan's Economy Grew So Fast: The Sources of
    Postwar Expansion. Washington, D.C.: Brookings
    Institution, 1976.

    The rapidity of Japan's economic growth after
    World War II is the subject of this book. It
    provides estimates of the sources of this growth
    and comparisons with other countries using growth
    accounting techniques developed by Denison. To a
    significant extent, Japan's extraordinary growth

was made possible by its economic backwardness in
comparison to the U.S. at the beginning of this
period. Detailed time series analyses are
provided for national income and employment,
factors of production, labor, and capital.
Additional deteminants of long-term growth are
examined along with advances in knowledge, the
reallocation of resources, and economies of scale.
Sources of differences in levels of output per
person are also analyzed along with the question
of whether Japan can maintain this high rate of
growth in coming decades.

77. Dore, Ronald Philip. Structural Adjustment in
    Japan, 1970-82. Employment, Adjustment, and
    Industrialisation 1. Geneva: International Labour
    Office, 1986.

    Taking the fact that all economies and societies
    are subject to pressures for change as a given,
    this study attempts to find out how different
    countries adjust to these pressures. There are
    studies of each of the five largest developed
    countries of the West, which consider to what
    extent their adjustment to change is the result of
    particular policies, structural features, or the
    behavior of the work force. A key role in the
    study is occupied by Japan, because it has
    undergone change very thoroughly and caused
    changes to be felt in the other countries.
    Japan's success can be seen as the result of the
    collaboration of its government with private
    enterprise in setting up its industrial structure,
    the capacity of industrial policy to influence the
    economy, and the flexibility of the workers in
    accepting fluctuations in their earnings and
    working time.

78. Ehrlich, Eva. Japan, a Case of Catching-Up.
    Budapest: Akademiai Kiado, 1984.

    An historical overview is provided of Japanese
    industrialization since 1880 until 1974 (end of
    data.) The study focuses on the labor force and
    productivity, capital formation and utilization,
    changes in production and its structure, foreign
    trade, and Japan as a model of bipolar
    industrialization. It contains more than 50
    figures and 65 statistical tables.

79. Hadley, Eleanor M. Antitrust in Japan. Princeton,
    N.J.: Princeton University Press, 1970.

    This book studies the process of breaking up the
    concentrated businesses in the immediate postwar
    period, and the restructuring of the 1960's.

Dissolution of combines is examined in detail, including documentation of ownership ties and the legislation that was used to achieve the changes. Business groupings and concentrations are then analyzed for the more recent era. An assessment of the postwar performance of the Japanese economy is offered.

80. Hall, Robert B.,Jr. <u>Japan: Industrial Power of Asia</u>. Searchlight Books. Princeton, N. J.: D. Van Nostrand Co., 1963.

This book is written by a geography professor, with the aim of providing the background for an understanding of the Japanese industrial progress since the war. It offers a profile of the land, natural resources, climate, and geo-political conditions which influence Japan today. Agriculture, industry, and urbanization are described. The demographics of Japan are explored, and a brief account of trade and diplomatic relations is offered. It gives an overview of the changes in Japan from a traditional to a modern society.

81. Hirschmeier, Johannes, and Tsunehiko Yui. <u>The Development of Japanese Business, 1600-1980</u>. 2nd ed. London: George Allen & Unwin, 1981.

With the view that the role of big business in Japan's progress has been significant, though not always praise-worthy ethically, this book examines the history of Japan since 1600. The leadership of Japan is a major emphasis of the whole treatise. Postwar developments include the socio-economic conditions, postwar executives and their achievements, organization and management, and the value changes that have occurred.

82. Horiuchi, Akiyoshi. "The `Low Interest Rate Policy´ and Economic Growth in Postwar Japan." <u>The Developing Economies</u>. 22.4 (Dec. 1984): 349-371.

Rapid growth in the Japanese postwar economy is noted, and the conventional view, that the low interest rate policy was effective in attaining financial allocation favorable to rapid economic growth is criticized. Statistical data and analyses suggest that this view lacks a solid foundation. Interest rates themselves are traced, and other considerations are introduced.

83. Hunsberger, Warren S. <u>Japan: New Industrial Giant</u>. American-Asian Educational Exchange, Monograph Series 10. New York: American-Asian Educational

Exchange, 1972.

This book gives a background description of
Japan´s economic growth, covering the major
characteristics of its economic development.
Domestic and international trends are outlined, in
production and consumption. The political
ramifications of Japanese growth on the Asian
region are discussed. Predictions for the future
include a change in the heretofore low profile of
the Japanese internationally. And modifications
in the relations of Japan with China and the U.S.
can be expected.

84. Japan Economic Research Center. The Future of
World Economy and Japan. Tokyo: Japan Economic
Research Center, 1975.

This volume deals with projections and general
trends that can be seen based on present
actualities. Japan´s position in the world
economy is outlined. Domestic and international
issues are discussed.

85. Japan Economic Research Center. The Japanese
Economy in 1985: The Economic Environment
Surrounding Japanese Enterprise. Tokyo: Japan
Economic Research Center, 1976.

This book treats the future role of the Japanese
firm, domestically and internationally. It is
based on statistics from 1975, with projections
for the next ten years. More stable growth is
shown, and industrial restructuring is predicted.
The economic environment is outlined.

86. "Japanese Industry: The Unsteady Road to Recovery."
Japanese Finance and Industry. 35 (July/Sept.
1977): 10-20.

A review is given of Japanese industry in 1976,
outlining GNP and demand growth since the oil
crisis and showing production trends. Profit
comparisons are made with U.S. industries. The
economic outlook for 1977 is sketched with
industrial policy recommendations.

87. "Japan´s Industrial Structure - A Long Range
Vision, 1977 Edition; The Tasks for Attaining the
Goal of Sustainable Growth and the Direction of
Industrial Policy." News from MITI. 140 (10
Aug. 1977): 1-27.

Changes in the growth mechanism are discussed in
light of evolving international economic
relations. The effects of the current recession

on business spending and corporate earnings are
examined with proposed policies for averting an
excessive drop in business investment. Various
industrial groups will have to adjust to the
changing economic environment. Energy policy is
reviewed.

88. Kaneko, Yukio. "Changes in Japan's Industrial
    Structure since the Oil Crisis." The Developing
    Economies. 18.4 (Dec. 1980): 484-501.

    The purpose of this paper is to analyze the
    industrial adjustment process of manufacturing
    industries in Japan since the first oil crisis.
    There is a description of the macroscopic outlook
    and change in manufacturing industries. Factors
    that have made possible such adjustments, using
    the "degree of dependency of production of each
    sector on each item of final demand" on the basis
    of the Leontief model. The adjustment that has
    occurred is put into relief through analyzing the
    factors of change in the industrial structure
    using a model formulated on the basis of the
    Leontief model.

89. Kawata, Tadashi. "The Japanese Economic
    Disequilibrium." The Developing Economies. 13.4
    (Dec. 1975): 3-20.

    High growth and the emergence of large
    corporations in the context of a severely ailing
    world economy has set up conditions for Japan in
    which there is a disequilibrium in the economy. A
    disaffection of the people from the business world
    has been evident as a result of the way in which
    high growth has been achieved. Difficulties in
    the economy, especially concerning agriculture and
    energy are noted. The task of restoring
    equilibrium is described. This is to be achieved
    with greater national welfare, and by moving away
    from the big business system and toward a
    decentralized system.

90. Kitamura, Hiroshi. Choices for the Japanese
    Economy. London: Royal Institute of International
    Affairs (Distributed by Humanities), 1976.

    The author views the present Japanese position as
    standing on the edge of a turning point, with many
    vital problems of social and economic importance
    developing. On the domestic side, there are
    topics such as growth and development patterns,
    planning for social welfare of the population,
    inflation, and restructuring needed at the end of
    the "economic miracle" period. For the
    international aspect of Japan's position, the

author considers factors such as international
payments, differing growth rates and balancing of
trade. Trade adjustments are discussed, in terms
of the discriminatory policies of Japan,
protectionism, and prospects for trade expansion.
Financial issues are also treated, including the
capital flows, foreign economic aid, and foreign
investment trends.

91. Klein, Lawrence, and Kazushi Ohkawa, eds. Economic
    Growth: The Japanese Experience since the Meiji
    Era, Proceedings of an International Conference on
    Economic Growth, 1st, Tokyo, 1966. Homewood,
    Ill.: Irwin, 1986.

    Papers from this conference centered on two
    topics: economic growth in historical
    perspective, and particular aspects of postwar
    growth. Long-term growth and structural changes
    are discussed, with a mechanism hypothesized for
    the acceleration swings. Monetary characteristics
    of growth are then taken up. Manufacturing's
    pattern of growth is then outlined, with the role
    of technological progress as one of the factors
    underlying the pattern. Foreign trade and its
    role in economic growth is followed through the
    prewar years. Private consumption is traced. In
    regard to the factors making possible the strong
    growth in the postwar period, papers are offered
    on the following themes: data which characterize
    the growth pattern; rapid industrialization's
    domestic patterns and manufacturing sector
    changes; heavy industrialization; and public
    sector policies and influence.

92. Komiya, Ryutaro, ed. Postwar Economic Growth in
    Japan. Trans. Robert S. Ozaki. Berkeley:
    University of California Press, 1966.

    Rapid growth of the Japanese economy has been
    accompanied by some important structural shifts
    and changes in income distribution. The difference
    in wages between the highest and lowest paid
    employees has narrowed slightly. Real consumption
    levels are growing. Problems such as inflation,
    housing shortages, and traffic congestion have
    come with the rapid changes. This collection of
    essays treats the public finance and monetary
    policy, balance of payments, income distribution
    and savings, business fluctuations and
    stabilization policy, and management policy.

93. Kosai, Yutaka. The Era of High-Speed Growth: Notes
    on the Postwar Japanese Economy. Trans.
    Jacqueline Kaminski. Tokyo: University of Tokyo
    Press, 1986.

This book gives a chronological account of the
postwar economic developments in Japan. It offers
explanations of the causes of the rapid growth and
the recent slowdown. Topics of interest include
the immediate postwar period, and causes of the
discontent of the 1960s, as well as the pace of
the liberalization and the bureaucratic mistakes
and corruption. Statistical background is ample.
The translation of a work originally published in
1981, this book contains data up to 1978.

94. Kosai, Yutaka, and Yoshitaro Ogino. The
    Contemporary Japanese Economy. Trans. Ralph
    Thompson. Armonk, N.Y.: Sharpe, 1984.

    A synopsis of a book published in 1980, this work
    discusses macroeconomic trends in Japan since the
    Second World War. The higher growth up until 1970
    and moderate growth in the period since 1970 are
    traced. High savings, and changes in the business
    cycles´ patterns, along with capital accumulation
    rates are the main items of focus. Attention is
    also given to the microeconomic adjustments in the
    Japanese economy, as growth rates have slowed.
    This has had an effect on the smaller firms, as
    has the liberalization of financial regulations.
    The social and political aspects of Japan´s
    economic system are also reviewed. The view that
    government officials excercise domination is
    rebutted, and the role of various complementary
    groups is outlined.

95. Kurihara, Kenneth K. The Growth Potential of the
    Japanese Economy. Baltimore: Johns Hopkins Press,
    1971.

    This book analyzes the factors that permit and
    retard Japanese economic growth. Beginning with
    the highlights of the "miracle" since the War, the
    role of demilitarization is first examined. The
    structure of industry also affects growth, as
    heavy industries are favored. Consumption and
    saving patterns are then treated, showing that the
    consuming public has not tightened its belt as
    savings patterns have changed. Now that stable
    growth is Japan´s goal, not merely rapid growth,
    new patterns of investment are emerging. The
    supply of labor can pose problems if anticipated
    shortages are not overcome. A special fiscal and
    monetary milieu is required, and technological
    gains are also key. Finally, analyses are offered
    for the economic growth of Japan without secular
    inflation, and for the balance of payments under
    sustained growth.

96. Leggatt, Timothy. The Evolution of Industrial

Systems: The Forking Paths. London: Croom Helm, 1985.

It is argued that evolutionary change characterizes modern industrial systems. General theories of industrial development are offered. Then treatment of Japan and the U.S.S.R., as two countries recently to emerge from the undeveloped state to modern industrial economies, is given, with attention to the history of each. Issues of control of corporate power, the automation of the workplace and shift to service economies are important for capitalist systems. Japanese industry is examined from its development through World War II, and then the Japanese Way is outlined.

97. Lockwood, William W., ed. The State and Economic Enterprise in Japan: Essays in the Political Economy of Growth. Conference on Modern Japan of the Association for Asian Studies. Princeton, N.J.: Princeton University Press, 1965.

These essays study Japan´s rapid economic modernization since 1868. The first half concentrates on the Meiji Era, 1886-1911, when the foundations of a modern industrial society and modern state were established. The second half analyzes Japan´s explosive economic development since World War II. In this section, Japan´s "new capitalism" is discussed with a look at cyclical instability and fiscal-monetary policy. In additional, regional planning, the labor market and politics, and Japan´s income-doubling plan are covered.

98. Macrae, Norman. "Must Japan Slow?" Economist. 274.7121 (23 Feb. 1980): 3-42.

A review is given of economic, social, and political development of Japan. Focus centers on the perceived need of the Japanese economy to maintain an accelerated rate of growth. The industrial policy of Japan´s Ministry of International Trade and Industry is examined along with general economic policy, foreign policy, and public administration.

99. Maddison, Angus. Economic Growth in Japan and the USSR. New York: Norton, 1969.

In a basic history of the economic growth of Japan and the U.S.S.R., the two countries are contrasted and compared with the other industrialized nations. Both started out the last century relatively backward, and made great progress, but

along different paths. The government had a
significant role in economics for both. And they
have managed to narrow the gap between rich and
poor, unlike any other nations today. The
spending on education and investment which helped
to produce the success of Japan and the U.S.S.R.
was considerable, and to catch up with the
developed world some sacrifice in consumption was
needed. Japan and the U.S.S.R. differ markedly in
the rates of export and the postwar military
spending rates. The impact of wars over the
century has heavily affected the phasing of
growth. The comparison of the U.S.S.R. and the
U.S., just like the comparison of Japan and the
U.S., can often lead to overstatements, because
the U.S. has such a different set of starting
points. On the other hand, the U.S.S.R.-Japan
comparison yields many fruitful insights which
help in the understanding of today´s developing
economies elsewhere in the world.

100. Mahajan, V. S. Development Planning: Lessons from
Japanese Model. Calcutta: Minerva Associates,
1976.

This book argues that there are features in the
Japanese model which the rest of the world might
well emulate. The history of military rule in
Japan is recounted and its influence in developing
the Japanese economy is emphasized. The pattern
of economic growth is traced, family loyalty is
examined as a factor which affected the system of
creation of capital in Japan, and the role of
military policies is traced. Conclusions are
offered.

101. Minami, Ryoshin. The Economic Development of
Japan: A Quantitative Study. Studies in the
Modern Japanese Economy. New York: St. Martin´s
Press, 1987.

This study of Japanese economic development covers
the years 1880 to the present. Topics considered
include the role of agriculture during the
industrialization period, the industrialization
process, capital formation, foreign trade,
population and labor demographics, the financial
system, prices and living standards, and future
prospects that can be anticipated. The chapters
are detailed and summaries are provided.
Statistical information is copious. The economics
of development and policies for the encouraging of
development are treated.

102. Minami, Ryoshin. The Turning Point in Economic
Development: Japan´s Experience. Tokyo:

Kinokuniya Bookstore, 1973.

The process of economic growth in less developed
countries requires a "turning point" theory to
explain its progress, it is argued. The theory is
presented and Japan's case is related to the
theory. Key concepts include the supply price of
labor and the wage level in the subsistance
sector. Mathematical forms of the theory are
applied.

103. Miyazaki, Yoshikazu. "Big Corporations and
Business Groups in Postwar Japan." The Developing
Economies. 14.4 (December 1976): 381-401.

This paper is in two parts, the first using
statistics to measure economic strength in Japan's
big corporations and business groups, then
elucidating postwar development and making a
comparison of present-day to prewar strength. The
second attempts to delimit in statistical terms
trends in the gradually rising cash-flow ratio in
these big corporations and business groups and to
shed some light on their implications. Results of
the rising cash-flow ratios are likely to be a
greater incidence of control of one corporation
over another, and a reduction of the influence of
the shareholders of corporations, with a
corresponding loss of balance of powers in the
economy. There is also a tendency for the balance
between household savings and investment to be
interrupted by such high levels of cash
accumulated by the corporations.

104. Miyazaki, Yoshikazu. "Rapid Economic Growth in
Post-War Japan: With Special Reference to
`Excessive Competition´ and the Formation of
`Keiretsu´." The Developing Economies. 5.2 (June
1967): 329-350.

The rapid economic growth of post-war Japan is
analyzed from three points of view: the
acquisition of investment funds by enterprises,
the investment behavior of enterprises, and the
role of the government. It is noted that the
economy, after the dissolution of the pre-war
zaibatsu, has passed through a unique
reorganization process. In this process there has
been excessive competition among firms. This
competition has resulted in high growth
tendencies.

105. Mizoguchi, Toshiyuki. "High Personal Saving Rate
and Changes in the Consumption Pattern in Postwar
Japan." The Developing Economies. 8.4 (Dec.
1970): 407-426.

This paper analyzes why the rate of personal
saving in Japan is high by international
standards, and how its rate continues to move
upward. Real per capital personal income
increased by 400 per cent in the period from 1953
to 1968. And yet the rate of personal consumption
has been revolutionized. Various factors are
identified which could account for the high rate
of personal savings.

106. Morishima, Michio. Why Has Japan Succeeded?:
Western Technology and the Japanese Ethos.
Cambridge: Cambridge University Press, 1982.

This book is written from a viewpoint in harmony
with that of Max Weber. It is argued that the
Japanese national experience, in addition to its
religious and cultural values, have contributed
significantly to the development of its economic
system. The book details the cultural and
economic development of Japan since the sixth
century. Changes brought about by the pressure
from the Chinese empire and later on by advances
of the Western powers are explained. The Taikai
reforms (645-49) and the Meyi revolution (1867-68)
which followed the changes are treated.
Development of the economy since early times is
outlined. An explanation based on the Japanese
ethos is offered for the development of the
strategy which enabled Japan to catch up with the
countries of the West. Statistics are offered
covering the years 1909-1977.

107. Nakamura, Takafusa. The Postwar Japanese Economy:
Its Development and Structure. Trans. Jacqueline
Kaminski. Tokyo: University of Tokyo, 1981.

Attempting to give an explanation of Japanese
growth since 1945, this book offers background
information on the prewar economic structure.
Then there is a description of the means of rapid
growth, its mechanisms, policies, "dual"
structures of large and small firms, and the
agricultural system. The change in growth rate
from rapid to stable is also described. The
explanation offered for the progress of Japan owes
much to its understanding of the prewar situation,
the reforms immediately after the war, and the
concerted actions of the Japanese themselves.

108. Nakamura, Takafusa, and Bernard R. G. Grace.
Economic Development of Modern Japan. Tokyo?:
Ministry of Foreign Affairs, 1985.

This book offers an overview of the Japanese
economic history, including early periods.

Changes in industrial structure are followed, with two chapters which focus on the developments since 1951. Those deal with the pace of growth, conditions giving rise to growth, and government policy roles. Fiscal and monetary measures are treated. The dual economic structure is analyzed. Then the discussion turns to period in which rapid growth ended, with the oil crisis and the advent of stable growth.

109. Nakayama, Ichiro. <u>Industrialization of Japan</u>. Tokyo: Centre for East Asian Cultural Studies, 1963.

The causes of the rapid growth of Japan´s economy are assessed in relation to the characteristics of traditional society. Rather than seeing tradition as a brake on the progress of industrialization, the author views it as "happy marriage between traditional society and modern industrialization." Postwar growth factors are uncovered. The nature of Japanese tradition is explored, and long-range factors supporting growth are described.

110. Namiki, Nobuyoshi. "The Industrial Structure of Japan in the 1980s." <u>The Developing Economies</u>. 18.4 (Dec. 1980): 502-521.

This article emphasizes the role of postwar rationalization and modernization, as well as the role of rationalization as it continues into the 1980´s. All sectors, from manufacturing to services, are seen as modernizing in their own patterns. Rapid modernization and its prerequisites are traced. The growing and receding industries are then compared. Other topics are considered.

111. Nomura Research Institute and Financial Times. <u>Prospects for Japanese Industry to 1985</u>. 2 vols. Management Reports. London: Financial Times, 1979.

This report analyzes the development of the Japanese industry, providing statistical coverage for the 1960-1985 period. It discusses changes in industrial structure and industrial policy. Reviews of major industries are covered: paper, pulp, iron, steel, machinery, shipbuilding, automobiles, petrochemicals, construction, precision instruments, computers, pharmaceuticals, food, fashion, leisure, and retailing. Supply and demand conditions of various markets are described along with developments in foreign trade.

112. Ohkawa, Kazushi, and Henry Rosovsky. "Japanese

Economic Development: Recent Japanese Growth in
Historical Perspective." American Economic
Review. 53.2 (May 1963): 578-588.

The factors which account for the rapid economic
growth in Japan from 1953 to 1960 are
investigated. Figures on the sectoral composition
of the national product are offered. Observations
are made, and increases in the labor force, along
with shifts in the industrial structure seem to
hold a key role. Factors within the economy which
made these changes occur are sought. Incentives,
price stability, savings and other issues are
described.

113. Ohkawa, Kazushi, and Henry Rosovsky. Japanese
     Economic Growth: Trend Acceleration in the
     Twentieth Century. Stanford, Calif.: Stanford
     University Press, 1973.

     This book is a compendium on the growth of the
     Japanese economy and the measurement of this
     trend. Background and changes since the Meiji
     Restoration are offered. Modern growth and its
     contours are outlined, with description of trends
     and swings, and the capitalization and structure
     of the economy. Factor inputs and aggregate
     productivity measures are given. The relation of
     the industrial sectors and agriculture is
     examined. Labor patterns, with the dualistic
     structure and wage differentials are explored.
     Aggregate demand and resource allocation are then
     described, showing the investment, consumption and
     production interchange. Foreign trade is
     characterized, and then a set of conclusions are
     offered regarding the economics of trend
     acceleration, the institutions in Japan, and the
     future prospects.

114. Ohkawa, Kazushi, et al., eds. Patterns of
     Japanese Economic Development: A Quantitative
     Appraisal. New Haven: Yale University Press,
     1979.

     This is an important statistical reference work
     which covers Japan's economic growth. The problem
     of how to define a set of economic statistics for
     Japan has been undertaken, with national product
     and expenditure figures as the key aim. The
     composition of gross national product changes over
     time, as the economy develops, adding complexity
     to an already difficult task. Results are
     interpreted accordingly by the authors. Growth
     rates are analyzed, production structure is
     measured, and agricultural output is traced.
     Product allocation and factor shares, prices and

population are also given in-depth analysis.

115. Okawa, Kazushi. Differential Structure and
     Agriculture: Essays on Dualistic Growth. Economic
     Research Series 13, Institute of Economic
     Research, Hitotsubashi University. Tokyo:
     Kinokuniya Bookstore, 1972.

     Essays not previously available in English are
     presented. The issue of "dualistic growth" in
     which the historical process changes both the
     modern and traditional enterprises, leaving the
     dualism intact, is examined. The pattern of long-
     term economic growth is explored. The
     differentials in employment structure, wages,
     productivity and prices are described. There is
     also a consideration of the labor supply picture
     and the status of agriculture.

116. Okawa, Kazushi. The Growth Rate of the Japanese
     Economy Since 1878. Tokyo: Kinokuniya Bookstore,
     1957.

     This historical survey reports on growth rates for
     the Japanese economy for the last 100 years.
     Statistical data are given with analysis. Some
     information on the recent period is offered.
     Implications and causal explanations are outlined.

117. Okawa, Kazushi, and Nobukiyo Takamatsu. Capital
     Formation, Productivity and Employment: Japan´s
     Historical Experience and Its Possible Relevance
     to LDCS. IDCJ Working Paper Series 26. Tokyo:
     International Development Center of Japan, 1983.

     Japan´s long-term economic development is analyzed
     in terms of the relationship among capital
     formation, productivity, and employment. A simple
     framework using a total productivity concept is
     applied to study the empirical relations between
     these factors. Japan´s development is
     characterized by "dualistic growth", where the
     industrial sector represents the modern sector and
     agriculture the traditional one. The relevance of
     Japan´s historical experience to LDCs is
     discussed, while focusing on the problem of
     development plan formulation and making long-term
     perspective.

118. Okita, Saburo. Causes and Problems of Rapid
     Growth in Postwar Japan and their Implications for
     Newly Developing Economies. Japan Economic
     Research Center Paper 6. Tokyo: Japan Economic
     Research Center, 1967.

     Observations on the remarkable postwar growth of

the Japanese economy are made. Its causes are
identified, including the postwar recovery
measures and reforms. The role of militarism is
examined. The origins of the semi-backward
economic structure which preceded rapid growth,
are explored. Politics and attitudes are
discussed. There is also a treatment of the
international environment.

119. Okita, Saburo. The Developing Economies and
Japan: Lessons in Growth. Tokyo: University of
Tokyo Press, 1980.

This book is a collection of essays on the
developing economies, primarily those of Asia, and
the role of the Japanese economic model as an aid
to these countries. Though Japan is now an
advanced economy, its recent transformation may
place it in a position to teach its own experience
to the now rapidly developing nations elsewhere in
Asia. Transfer of resources to developing
countries should be sought. Some problems and
their causes are identified, and the importance of
population trends for development is assessed.
Economic planning is examined, and the diplomacy
of recent years is recounted. Japan's role in
ASEAN is considered, both in terms of conflicts
and interdependence.

120. Okuda, Yoshio. Japan's Postwar Industry. Tokyo:
International Society for Educational Information,
1976.

The postwar recovery of the Japanese economy is
explored by a thorough examination of the various
industries and their developmental patterns.
Implications of government policy are treated,
with the private sector role also in view.

121. Organisation for Economic Cooperation and
Development. Japan. O.E.C.D. Economic Survey.
Paris: OECD, 1964-.

This annual report provides descriptions and
details of developments in the Japanese economy.
Macroeconomic factors, such as, demand and output,
employment and the labor market, prices, incomes,
and balance of payments are discussed and
analyzed. Reviews are also given of governmental
policies, including monetary and fiscal,
industrial, and energy. In addition, commentaries
on short-term prospects, foreign trade, regional
conditions, and international comparisons are
offered.

122. Ozaki, Iwao. "Industrial Structure and

Employment: The Experiences in Japanese Economic Development, 1955-68." The Developing Economies. 14.4 (December 1976): 341-365.

There is a mutual dependence between the industrial structure and the pattern of industrial development promoted by the Japanese government. This paper attempts to provide a comprehensive description of interrelations among patterns of industrial development, technological characteristics, the changes over time in production and demand conditions, the effects of the government's industrial policies, and the employment structure, on the basis of the experiences of the Japanese economy from 1955 to 1968. Topics include technology types, resource allocation, commodity classification, demand, exports, and employment. Certain sectors of the technology and commodity classification are shown to have high impact on employment.

123. Patrick, Hugh, ed. Japanese Industrialization and Its Social Consequences. Berkeley: Univeristy of California Press, 1976.

This treatment of the social conditions of the Japanese industrial work force consists of 12 papers. The special status of the industrial as opposed to the nonindustrial workers is noted frequently, and the issue of the difference between conditions in large vs. small firms also recurs as a theme. The large/small dualism is observed to be a complex phenomenon, with many non-economic factors. Wage differentials are described and a number of plausible causes, beyond the strictly economic, are proposed. Lifestyles of workers in the different sectors are compared, with attention to female industrial workers and to male mine workers, representing groups with special problems. Three industries are compared, cotton-spinning, shipbuilding, and general trading companies. Some general conclusions as to the profound changes in Japanese society as a result of industrialization are made.

124. Patrick, Hugh, and Henry Rosovsky, eds. Asia's New Giant: How the Japanese Economy Works. Washington, D.C.: Brookings Institution, 1976.

In a comprehensive text which deals with the Japanese economy, the data which documents Japan's development since the war is presented and analyzed. Topics include the following: Japan's economic performance, an overview; economic growth and its sources; fiscal, monetary and related policies; banking and finance; taxation; Japan and

the world economy; industrial organization;
technology; labor market; urbanization and urban
problems; politics, government and economic
growth; social and cultural factors in Japanese
economic growth; and prospects for the future.
With each topic research results are given, and
analysis of data is offered.

125. Pempel, T. J. Policy and Politics in Japan:
Creative Conservatism. Policy and Politics in
Industrial States. Philadelphia: Temple
University Press, 1982.

Since the end of World War II, the conservative
Liberal Democratic Party (LDP) has dominated
Japanese politics. But unlike other ruling
conservative parties, the LDP has adapted to new
circumstances and built Japan into an
international political and economic power. This
study examines the LDP´s policies and responses to
the changing domestic and international
environment. It concentrates on economic policy,
labor-management relations, social welfare, higher
education, environmental protection, and
administrative reform.

126. "Priorities in Japan´s International Trade and
Industry Policy for Fiscal Year 1980." News from
MITI. 214 (Sept. 27, 1979): 1-9.

An analysis is given of Japan´s foreign trade
policy and industrial policy for the fiscal year
1980. Additional topics include energy policy,
international cooperation, technological
development, stimulation of medium and small
firms, industrial location, and occupational
safety.

127. Shinohara, Miyohei. "Causes and Patterns in the
Postwar Growth." The Developing Economies. 8.4
(Dec. 1970): 349-368.

Characteristics of economic growth in postwar
Japan are described. The high growth due to
rehabilitation factors has continued and may well
allow Japan to surpass Western countries even in
per capital income level. Unbalanced fixed
investment is a clear trait in the economy. The
"Schumpeterian" process in which "over-loan" and
technological innovation interact has been
operating to guarantee the rapid growth. Active
interfirm competition and the role of the MITI are
discussed. Now a labor-deficient condition
exists, and the economy has shifted from a foreign
reserves lack to a condition of surplus foreign
reserves. To prevent inflation, this indicates a

need to liberalize trade and foreign exchange rates.

128. Shinohara, Miyohei. <u>Growth and Cycles in the Japanese Economy</u>. Tokyo: Kinokuniya Bookstore, 1962.

This book ascertains the statistical characteristics of the growth of the Japanese economy and then seeks to discover the reasons for the high rate of growth. Factors explored include postwar recovery features, export growth potentials, and the effect of the concentration of capital in large firms. The dual structure and the existence of Kuznetz cycle are treated, and the dynamic mechanism for cyclic growth is explored. The structure of savings and consumption functions, income multipliers and the marginal propensity to invest are also considered.

129. Shinohara, Miyohei. <u>Industrial Growth, Trade, and Dymanic Patterns in the Japanese Economy</u>. Tokyo: University of Tokyo, 1982.

This book is divided into three parts. Part I reviews Japan's postwar industrial development, examining structures unique to Japan and the industrial policies of the Ministry of International Trade and Industry. In addition, business groups and the coalition of parent companies and their subsidiaries are analyzed as a peculiar aspect of the Japanese business community. Part II studies from an historical perspective the factors which contributed to the sharp and sustained increases in Japan's exports and the drastic structural changes of its exports, as well as developing the "boomerang effect" to describe the interaction between the old and newly emerging industrial states. Part III looks at the dynamic patterns in growth and cycles in Japan's postwar period, examining its high savings ratio and re-examining Kondratieff, Juglar, and Kitchin cycles.

130. Shinohara, Miyohei. <u>Structural Changes in Japan's Economic Development</u>. Tokyo: Kinokuniya Bookstore, 1970.

As a companion to an earlier book, <u>Growth and Cycles in the Japanese Economy</u>, 1962, this volume is a delineation in statistical terms of the growth of the Japanese economy and the structural changes which have accompanied that growth. The original data have been extended, and certain economic variables have been estimated on the basis of some new hypotheses. Numerous factors

which are useful in accounting for the fast growth
of Japan are traced. There are postwar factors
and more long-range factors. Savings and
investment behavior are investigated, and the
measurement of the Japanese growth rate in an
international perspective is attempted.
Structural changes are identified as long-term
processes. The dual economy, its regional
structure and its differentials are traced.

131. Simonis, Heide, and Udo Enrest Simonis, eds.
     Japan: Economic and Social Studies in
     Development. Wiesbaden: Otto Harrassowitz, 1974.

     This is a collection of essays with varied topics
     and points of view. For example, some
     consideration of how well the national welfare is
     represented by the gross national product concept
     is offered. There are presentations on the small
     and medium industries, collective bargaining,
     Japanese investment in foreign countries, trading
     companies, technology, the Pacific region,
     economic planning, and other diverse issues.
     There is also some examination of the impact of
     Japan´s rapid economic growth and its causes.

132. Stockwin, James A. Japan: Divided Politics in a
     Growth Economy. New York: W.W. Norton & Co.,
     1975.

     With political history as its background, this
     study offers an overview of the recent Japanese
     economy. Three important factors are identified,
     the stability of Liberal Democratic rule, the
     economic growth phenomenon, and the acute
     political division on fundamental issues. The
     success in government management of the strains
     between the factions is one of the key
     observations to be made. Without claiming to
     explain all the sources of division, this book
     describes the current situation in Japanese
     politics.

133. Stone, P. B. Japan Surges Ahead: The Story of an
     Economic Miracle. New York: Frederick A. Praeger,
     1969.

     This book is an overview of the Japanese economic
     miracle. The general causes for the recent
     success of Japan are sought, in a balanced picture
     which includes insights on the Japanese character.
     The nation is described and compared with others
     in its physical and social characteristics.
     Modern industrial sectors are examined.
     Technology and human factors are described.
     Conclusions are offered which summarize the

overall findings of the book.

134. Takahashi, Kamekichi. The Rise and Development of Japan's Modern Economy: The Basis for "Miraculous" Growth. Trans. John Lynch. Tokyo: Jiji Press, 1969.

With the view that Japan's remarkable growth is no miracle, but the result of 100 years of hard work, this book emphasizes the role of the early history of Japanese industrialization, and the Meiji period. The thesis is that the unleashing of the "warrior spirit" of the Meiji samurai class took place with the abolition of feudal restrictions. This ethic is seen as the driving force behind the present Japanese business success.

135. Tanaka, Kakuei. Building a New Japan: A Plan for Remodelling the Japanese Archipelago. Trans. Simul International. Tokyo: Simul Press, Inc., 1973; Tokyo: Nippon Retto Kaizo-Ron, 1972.

The original edition was published just before the author became Prime Minister of Japan, outlining a vision of the policy needs of the country. The rapid postwar growth of Japan brought with it many of the most difficult problems of urban societies, such as inflation, urban deterioration, pollution, stagnant agriculture, and the frustration of spiritual values amid affluence. Proposals for the institution of land use reforms, the formation of national information and communications networks, and international cooperation are offered. The book represents a blueprint for change.

136. Tsuru, Shigeto. Essays on Japanese Economy. Economic Research Series. Tokyo: Kinokuniya Bookstore, 1958.

This essay collection treats economic stability in postwar Japan. Financial and industrial sectors are examined. Foreign exchange rates in the postwar period are traced and analyzed. Employment and economic planning, as well as the effects of the Korean war on Japan are presented. A historical overview is offered.

137. Tsuru, Shigeto. "Growth and Stability of the Postwar Japanese Economy." American Economic Review. 51.2 (May 1961): 400-411.

This paper focuses on the reasons for the high rate of economic growth in Japan up to the end of 1960. Statistical indicators are summarized. Historical background is offered, with indications

of problems which held back growth. The solution
of each of the problems is discussed, in terms of
the shift in structure. High rates of profit and
investment are noted. Sources of high effective
demand are investigated. Other considerations and
future outlook are also covered.

138. Tsurutani, Takesugu. Political Change in Japan:
Response to Postindustrial Challenge. Comparative
Studies of Political Life. New York: D. McKay and
Co., 1977.

Japan's distinctive position as a country that is
very modern in socio-economic terms by not quite
modern in terms of politics is presented. There
is a demonstration of the ways in which Japan
differs from the Western nations, through its
closed society, the patron-client democracy, and
the vertical society organization patterns it
manifests. The concept of a postindustrial change
is modelled. As Japan has moved out of a typical
agrarian stage, through a modern industrial stage
and further into a more modern form, there have
been responses in the political institutions which
often do not keep up with the pace of change. New
issues are identified for the future.

139. Uchino, Tatsuro. Japan's Postwar Economy: An
Insider's View of Its History and Its Future.
Trans. Mark A. Harbison. Tokyo: Kodansha
International (Distributed by Harper & Row), 1983;
Tokyo: Sengo Nihon keizaishi, 1978.

Offering a recent economic history of Japan, this
work is written from a viewpoint which attempts
objectivity, neither supporting nor opposing the
policies of the Japanese government. Political
and social trends are noted along with the
economic development. Chronological organization
of the work proceeds as follows: the immediate
postwar period, from 1945-50, during which every
economic sector was operating below pre-war
levels. The Korean War period, from 1950-55, saw
the Japanese economy recover its independence.
The Technology/Mass Consumer period from 1955-59
was when the high level investment started. The
High Speed Growth period, in the early 60's,
brought the full employment economy. The
Superpower state, from the early 1960's to 1971
was characterized by continued growth and the
advent of problems with pollution. The End of
Rapid Growth came in 1971, and through 1983 the
global economy experienced several shocks and
structural imbalances.

140. Valery, N. "Japan: A Survey." Economist.

288.7297 (July 9, 1983): 1-12.

The economic and social development of Japan is traced. Information on the import and export picture for manufacturing is given, along with demographic changes in Japan. Wholesalers and shops' contribution is analyzed, as well as the importance of small business. Industrial policy is discussed, capital investment and exports are described, and the status of competition with the U.S. is given. Five stages of technological development are offered. The potential of women workers is also estimated.

141. Williams, D. Beyond Political Economy. Berlin: East Asian Institute, Free University of Berlin, 1983.

This brief volume gives a critique of issues raised in Chalmers Johnson's MITI and the Japanese Miracle. The question of the role of policy in Japan's economic growth is debated.

142. Woronoff, Jon. Japan: The Coming Economic Crisis. Tokyo: Lotus Press, 1979.

While admitting the extraordinary accomplishments of Japan, this work examines the often forgotten negative effects of that achievement. Not a "miracle," the Japanese growth and recovery has been won at a considerable cost. The historical and cultural background to Japanese economic success is recounted. The structure of the economy is outlined. The keys to rapid development and the obstacles are identified. Some of the important values of the old way of life have been lost, and there are difficulties in maintaining the values which have resulted in the new high growth economy. Negative reactions from Japan's trading partners are described. Possibilities for the future are outlined.

143. Woronoff, Jon. The Japan Syndrome: Symptoms, Ailments, and Remedies. New Brunswick, N.J.: Transaction Books, 1986.

From a critic of Japan, this work attempts to suggest ways for Japan to remedy the criticisms. Portions of the book have already appeared as articles. At times polemic, the book signals the end of the great Japanese productivity boom. Trouble in industry and with labor is described. Problems with maintaining exports and financial stability are outlined. Inadequacies of policies are discussed. Remedies include looking toward new materials, biotechnology and communications

industries. Improved housing and wage increases
are suggested. Reforms and new goals are urged.

144. Yamamoto, Noboru. The Modernization of the
     Economy and Postwar Expansion. Tokyo:
     International Society for Educational Information,
     1973.

     Offering an overview of recent economic history in
     Japan, this book relates modern Japan to its
     traditions. Recent history is traced, and changes
     since the Second World War are pictured. Features
     of the economy are portrayed, including the dual
     structure, the expanding exports, and capital
     liberalization. The industrial structure and
     Japan´s position in the world economy are traced.

145. Yamamoto, Shuji. "Japan´s New Industrial Era: I.
     Restructuring Traditional Industries." Long Range
     Planning: International Journal of Strategic and
     Long Range Planning. 19.1 (Feb. 1986): 61-65.

     Expectations for the Japanese economy´s growth in
     the future are offered. With the adjustment to
     high oil prices having been made, Japan will be
     able to continue to grow unabated, focusing on the
     microelectonics technology and information and
     service-oriented industries. The private sector
     has sufficient vitality to offset the budgetary
     deficit with well-timed increased participation in
     infrastructural investment. A growth rate of 5%
     or more should be sustained for the next few
     years, with growth potential also to be expected
     in the Pacific basin region. It will be a
     challenge to Japan to bear its share of the
     leadership of the world economy in the coming
     years.

146. Yamamura, Kozo, ed. The Domestic Transformation.
     Vol 1 of The Political Economy of Japan.
     Stanford, Calif.: Stanford University Press, 1987.

     This volume will provide accurate descriptions of
     changes in Japan since 1945, analyses of the
     reasons for the performance of the political
     economy of postwar Japan, and realistic
     predictions for the immediate future. Special
     consideration is given to the period since 1973.

147. Yamazawa, Ippei. "Increasing Imports and
     Structural Adjustment of the Japanese Textile
     Industry." The Developing Economies. 18.4 (Dec.
     1980): 441-462.

     Structural adjustment is the process of moving to
     a new equilibrium after a change in economic

conditions, through market mechanisms or policy
intervention. Japanese adjustment in the 1970's
is explored as a response to the oil price shocks
and the disparity of growth performance among
developed countries. A structural depression was
caused by these factors. An overview of
structural adjustment during this period is given,
with special concern with the textile industry,
trade liberalization, and import policy. Other
factors are also included.

148. Yanaga, Chitoshi. <u>Big Business in Japanese
Politics</u>. New Haven: Yale University Press, 1968.

The rapid Japanese growth since the war was made
possible by the close cooperation of the
government and major industries. This study
examines the political basis of that cooperation.
The style and framework of the Japanese political
system is described. The participation of
business in the government is detailed. The role
of the bureaucracy and its leadership is examined.
Business had an important role in: the design of
the peace treaty, mutually beneficial reparations
plans, the merger of conservative political
parties, the atomic energy policy, forging the
partnership with the U.S., aiming for growth. The
years 1951-60 are the primary focus. Printed
materials, government documents and interviews
provide the data for the study.

149. Yoshitomi, Masaru. "The Recent Japanese Economy:
The Oil Crisis and the Transition to Medium Growth
Path." <u>The Developing Economies</u>. 14.3 (September
1976): p. 319-340.

The oil shock of 1973, though short-lived, was a
serious portent of difficulties for the Japanese
economy, with its three problems: price inflation,
economic recession, and a huge balance of payments
deficits. The increased prices for oil
exacerbated the inflation threat. Higher payments
for oil worsened the balance of payments
situation. The means for financing the balance of
payments in disequilibria is described. The
repercussions of the demand management policies
for an inflationary recession are traced. Policy
measures, recovery, and the narrow compass for the
selection of policy mix are discussed.
Conclusions are offered.

150. Youngson, A. J., ed. <u>Economic Development in the
Long Run</u>. New York: St. Martin's Press, 1973.

Japan is briefly covered in this collection which
offers nine papers presented at a conference held

in Edinburgh in September, 1971, on the topic of
"an understanding of the processes of development
which could be applied in some way to the problems
of poor countries today." Topics include natural
resources, technology, land ownership,
transportation, and human attitudes and behavior.

III. INTERNATIONAL COMPETITION AND INDUSTRIAL POLICY:
JAPAN AND THE UNITED STATES

A major portion of American literature on Japanese industrial policy centers on the success Japan has had in international markets. Consequently the United States has been forced to reconsider its position on industrial policy and its international competitiveness. Japan´s industrial policies are discussed in light of these considerations. Emphasis in this chapter is placed on the United States´ perspective and responses to Japan.

151. Abegglen, James C., and T. M. Hout. "Facing Up to the Trade Gap with Japan." Foreign Affairs. 57.1 (Fall 1978): 146-168.

An analysis is given of the U.S. trade deficit with Japan and the realities behind the U.S. competitive performance in Japan. The impact of the loss of the import market share on 1977 imports to Japan from the U.S. is examined. Differences in patterns of trade between the two countries is described, along with a review of the Japanese distribution system (its role as a barrier to market entry) and Japan´s industrial policy. Policy recommendations are offered for improving the U.S. position.

152. Andrews, Kenneth R., and Malcolm S. Salter. "The Automobile Crisis and Public Policy." Harvard Business Review. 59.1 (Jan./Feb. 1981): 73-82.

Philip Caldwell, chairman of Ford Motor Co., says the U.S. must adopt a national industrial policy to aid basic industries like the automobile industry. The government, business, labor, media, finance, and social elements need to make coordinated efforts to assist troubled industries. Meanwhile the government should impose import limits on Japanese autos and set up import quotas for individual countries. A strong industrial base is the foundation for high employment, national security, and better social conditions. An industrial policy should work through market-oriented, independent, profitable businesses. Regulatory and administrative policies should be

49

evaluated by their effects on industrial strength.
Public consensus is needed. Congress must develop
new policies, and new legislation should be
enacted.

153. "Antitrust, Industrial Policy, and `Technological
Predation´: The Myth of a Culture-Specific
Japanese Advantage (Part I)." Antitrust Law &
Economics Review. 16.4 (1984): 79-94.

Remarks of H. William Tanaka from an interview are
cited. His opinion is that the so-called "import
predation" in America is really just a version of
the improvement of technology to produce a
superior item at a lower cost. And while American
industries often do not experience heavy
competition on the domestic front, they must learn
to abandon old methods of production in favor of
newer and more cost-effective ones. What the
Japanese seem to appreciate is the truism that a
firm´s most important element is its work force.
Other observations include the recognition of the
importance of a quick response to consumer
preferences and a caution about the tendency of
government interference to lessen competitiveness
in the economy.

154. Baranson, Jack. The Japanese Challenge to U.S.
Industry. Lexington, Mass.: Lexington Books, D.C.
Heath and Co., 1981.

The strength of Japan as competitor to the U.S. in
trade and economic leadership is analyzed.
Factors identified include: the Japanese
capability to design and produce production
systems and manage them effectively, its high
quality labor force, the concern for cost
effectiveness and continual modernization of plant
and equipment, financial resources, and
government-industry cooperation. The U.S.
response patterns which have arisen in meeting
this challenge are characterized as rigid and
maladaptive. The U.S. firms tend to freeze their
product lines when confronted with Japanese
product superiority, and they move production to
low-wage facilities outside the U.S. rather than
developing a competitive high quality and low-cost
product. The U.S. firms tend to invest in less
sophisticated products, and to rely in excess on
trade restrictions as protection from Japanese
competition. And though some U.S. firms do keep
up with the Japanese challenge, most sectors of
industry are losing ground. This book is intended
as an assessment of the full nature of Japan´s
challenge, with the hope that better U.S.
responses can be found.

155. Barnds, William J., ed. <u>Japan and the United
     States: Challenges and Opportunities</u>. New York:
     New York University Press, 1979.

     A collection of essays by noted experts, this book
     describes the developments in the U.S.-Japanese
     relationship during the 1970's. Some of the
     reasons for a strain in the alliance are sought.
     The decline of America's relative military
     strength in the Pacific region, domestic
     developments in the two countries, and growing
     productivity in Japan are cited as factors. The
     nature of the trading disagreements between the
     Japanese and the Americans are analyzed. Some
     leading comments on the prospects for the future
     are offered in the context of the challenges that
     must be faced.

156. Bartel, Richard D. "Industrial Policy as an
     International Issue." <u>Challenge</u>. 23.6 (Jan./Feb.
     1981): 30-39.

     The industrial policy issue is discussed with
     William Diebold, Jr., Council of Foreign Relations
     in New York. Industrial policy is concerned with
     the structure of the economy and the term
     "industrial" is used in its broad sense to mean
     productive activity. Several strategies exist for
     an industrial policy: 1) a defensive policy to
     preserve the prevailing economic structure, 2) an
     adaptive policy to make structural adjustments,
     and 3) an innovative policy of initiating change
     rather than merely reacting to it. Industrial
     policy is an international issue because one
     nation's policy directly affects another's. The
     French Barre plan combined macroeconomic policies
     with the structural approach of an industrial
     policy. The U.S. needs an adaptive policy to
     continue a liberal trade policy.

157. Brown, William S. "Industrial Policy and
     Corporate Power." <u>Journal of Economic Issues</u>.
     19.2 (June 1985): 487-496.

     The nature of corporate power in the U.S.
     necessitates an industrial policy to increase
     aggregate productivity, income, and the flow of
     resources between industries. Labor and
     management power coalitions can by highly
     effective for increasing income shares. And
     special interest groups are self-seeking with
     social objectives in mind. A national industrial
     policy can provide social responsibility by
     coordinating incentives and subsidies. An
     effective industrial policy would consist of the
     following: 1) an income policy, 2) an economic

cooperation council, 3) a national investment
bank, 4) cooperative research and development, and
5) social accounting methods. The use of social
accounting methods is a crucial requirement to
prevent established power blocs from controlling
policy. The methods are useful for evaluating the
true costs and benefits of special interest
policies.

158. "Business Outlook Abroad: Japan." Business
America. 8.12 (June 10, 1985): 19-21.

Japan's Economic Planning Agency is forecasting
real growth of 4.6% for 1985 and sees private
capital investment increasing 8.5%. Also
predicted is a 1985 trade surplus of $44 billion,
while private sector forecasts exceed $55 billion.
The Reagan-Nakasone summit in January 1985 has
initiated talks of opening the Japanese market in
4 areas: telecommunications, electronics, forest
products, and medical and pharmaceutical products.
However Japan's industrial and trade policies
still hinder U.S. trade with Japan. Areas of
expanding opportunities in Japan for U.S. are raw
materials and agricultural goods, office machinery
and computers, electronic components, and
telecommunications equipment.

159. Cieply, Michael. "Do-It-Yourself Industrial
Policymaking." Forbes. 132.2 (July 18, 1983):
30-31.

This article covers the recent experiences of
William Kilkenny, chairman of Hyster Co., a
manufacturer of industrial lift trucks located in
Portland, Oregon. The demand for these trucks
varies with the economic cycles. From 1979 to
1982, net profits declined from $63 million to $7
million. Kilkenny believes that the recession is
not just to blame. Japanese competition is also
responsible. In addition to their manufacturing
skills, the Japanese rely on trade restrictions,
government cartels, and unfair subsidization.
Kilkenny's complaint typifies the reasons for a
new industrial policy. He has started his own
campaign by writting to 5 states and 4 nations in
which Hyster builds trucks asking them for aid in
keeping his plants open.

160. Cohen, Jerome B., ed. Pacific Partnership: United
States-Japan Trade, Prospects and Recommendations
for the Seventies. Lexington, Mass.: Lexington
Books, D.C. Heath, 1972.

The background of the U.S. balance of payments
deficits is explored, especially in relation to

Japan. The historical perspective and the impact of Japan's recent growth is offered. Price and cost comparisons for Japanese and American industries are outlined. The foreign trade pattern of Japan is examined, with its history and its future prospects. Direct foreign investments are discussed, and a treatment is given of the textile and auto industries. Conclusions are offered as to the competitiveness of Japan and the trade balance that might be achieved in the future. A reduction in Japan's reliance on the U.S. as a trade partner is likely, but it will be difficult for Japan to stand alone in the face of problems of international currency, balance of payments deficits and emergence of developing economies.

161. Cohen, Stephen S., and John Zysman. "Can America Compete?" Challenge. 29.2 (May/June 1986): 56-64.

The international economy is in a period of profound changes originating from 2 major forces: 1) changes in international competition and 2) changes in production technologies. The U.S.'s position in the international economic community is seriously threatened. American success depends on how well the U.S. learns to use knowledge to adjust to shifting markets and advancing technologies. Of primary importance is investment in human resources and in communities, not just engineers and scientists. A policy of dynamic adjustment to these forces must be formulated and prudent choices made.

162. Cole, Robert E. Work, Mobility, and Participation: A Comparative Study of American and Japanese Industry. Berkeley: University of California Press, 1979.

In a comparison of American and Japanese industry, this book examines key issues such as job mobility, the relationship between employer and employee in the decision-making process, and the work ethic. Case studies are used as the basis for the analysis, including date from studies of labor conditions in Detroit and Yokohama. The influence of the social, political and economic conditions in the different countries is examined. Conclusions are offered as to areas in which the U.S. could benefit from the Japanese model, the most important of these being in the career management and job security issues.

163. Cottrell, Alan. "The Undermining of British Industry." ESSO Magazine (UK). 113

(Winter/Spring 1980): 26-29.

Against the background of declining profits in
U.K. industry, the government's industrial policy
is blamed. Its anti-cyclical policies are the
main targets of criticism. Two models of
industrial policy are presented as alternatives:
the French-Japanese model involving government
intervention with real benefits to industry and
the German-American model which allows industries
to succeed or fail on their own. The latter
approach is recommended. The main components of
such an industrial policy are outlined.

164. Davidson, William H. The Amazing Race: Winning
the Technorivalry with Japan. New York: John
Wiley & Sons, 1984.

A description is given of the impact of U.S.-
Japanese competition on the developments in the
information technology sector and on the broader
social and economic conditions of both countries.
The first part of this book provides a
retrospective look at the origins of Japanese
industrial strategy, the workings of its economy,
and the American response during the years 1959-
1979. It then proceeds to examine the components
of the information technology sector, looking at
markets, competitive strategies, and basic
technology. In the final part, Japan's striving
to establish its preeminance in information
technology is discussed in the context of
government industrial policy, followed by the
response of U.S. industrial and goverment
policymakers, and the implications of this
competitive race for future development.

165. Denzau, Arthur T. Will an "Industrial Policy"
Work for the United States? Center for the Study
of American Business, Formal Publication 57. St.
Louis: Center for the Study of American Business,
Washington University, 1983.

This pamphlet raises the question of U.S.
industrial policy and focuses on the comparative
example of the Japanese system. The idea that
Japan's success has resulted from the industrial
policy it pursued is actually a myth, it is
argued. The ad hoc approach to U.S. industrial
policy is considered and its political basis
assessed. The report concludes with
recommendations that would provide employment and
growth benefits to the U.S. without the risk of
problems that would arise from adopting an
interventionist industrial policy.

166. Destler, I. M., and Hideo Sato, eds. Coping with
     U.S.-Japanese Economic Conflicts. Lexington,
     Mass.: Lexington Books, D.C. Heath and Co., 1982.

     This essay collection was planned as a study of
     the political/economic conflicts betwen the U.S.
     and Japan from 1977 to 1981. Five disputes are
     analyzed, by both American and Japanese experts,
     detailing difficulties in steel trade,
     automobiles, agricultural trade,
     telecommunications equipment, and macroeconomic
     policy coordination. The means by which these
     problems were resolved are examined. Some general
     matters are taken up, including prescriptions as
     to how officials can manage these problems more
     effectively.

167. Destler, I. M., et al. The Textile Wrangle:
     Conflict in Japanese-American Relations. Ithaca:
     Cornell University Press, 1979.

     In 1969 the Nixon Administration demanded the
     Japanese to place comprehensive controls on the
     sales of man-made fibre and wool textile products
     to the American market. The Japanese government
     failed to do so. For the next three years, this
     dispute dominated the economic relations between
     the two countries. This book seeks to explain how
     and why this happened from a political viewpoint.
     It looks inside the policy-making processes of
     both nations for the reasons why particular
     actions were taken, and why this dispute generated
     a broader political crisis.

168. Frank, Isaiah, ed. The Japanese Economy in
     International Perspective. Baltimore: Johns
     Hopkins University Press, 1975.

     This collection of essays was written against the
     background of Japan's phenomenal rate of economic
     growth, low rate of inflation, and growing
     balance-of-payment surpluses during the late
     1960's to 1972. At the same time, Japan
     experienced severe strains in its economic
     relations with other countries, especially the
     United States. These problems stemmed from a
     combination of three factors: 1. sharp increase in
     Japan's international competitiveness, 2. a set of
     foreign economic policies out of phase with
     Japan's economic strength, and 3. an international
     framework of institutions and rules incapable of
     adjusting to changes in the world economic
     community. Topics covered include: Japanese
     industrial policy, foreign trade, Japan's fiscal
     incentives for exports, Japanese foreign direct
     investment, and the international corporations.

169. Franko, Lawrence. The Threat of Japanese
     Multinationals: How the West Can Respond. New
     York: John Wiley & Sons, 1984.

     This book examines the reasons why the Japanese
     companies have been so sucessful in international
     markets. Contrary to the view that Japanese
     competitiveness resulted from the government's
     industrial policy, it is argued that success
     originated from the fierce competition within the
     Japanese market. The market forced research and
     development efforts toward commercial goals. The
     utilization of existing technology for marketable
     commodities was channelled through mass
     distribution systems. The twice yearly bonus
     system creates an important source of incentive
     for workers. The Japanese export their weaker
     industries and attempt to keep only those which
     are competitively stronger. The key to their
     success is strategic pragmatism, producing what
     the market wants, upgrading quality, and selling
     goods as cheaply as possible. These domestic
     market forces and strategies have produced Japan's
     international success. Case studies are given of
     how American companies that resemble Japanese
     companies have responded to the Japanese and won.
     The author advocates closer cooperation between
     American companies.

170. Gansler, Jacques S. "Defense: A `Demonstration
     Case' for Industrial Strategy." Challenge. 26.6
     (Jan./Feb. 1984): 58-61.

     U.S. monetary and fiscal policies have been
     ineffectual in dealing with the domestic economy
     and international competition. A coordinated
     industrial strategy is needed to encourage
     structural adjustments and to prevent any factors
     from slowing down these changes. Since the
     government has not engaged in this type of
     adjustment process before, the defense industry
     would be the one to demonstrate the value of an
     industrial policy. Policies would improve
     international competitiveness, reduce dependency,
     improve quality at lower prices, and optimize
     economic benefits from defense investments. The
     industrial policy of Japan is cited as a
     successful strategy for dealing with international
     competition.

171. Genovese, Frank C. "America's Economic Problems."
     Review of Business. 5.4 (Spring 1984): 26-30.

     The growing discussion in the U.S. over an
     industrial policy raises a number of questions: 1)
     What is an industrial policy? 2) What are the

problems in the U.S. economy? and 3) What are the
solutions? The primary concern should be for
raising the standard of living by organizing a
more efficient economic system. From 1960 to
1976, growth in real production per worker in the
U.S. lagged behind that of Japan, Italy, Germany,
France, and the U.K. From 1959 to 1976,
unemployment in the U.S. was higher than in these
countries. The loss of export markets and the
large volume of imports has been a focal point of
these industrial policy discussions. Recently
introduced legislative proposals should contribute
to these debates.

172. Gibney, Frank. Japan: The Fragile Superpower..
Rev. ed. New York: New American Library, Norton
Books, 1979.

Written to intepret the characteristics that have
made the Japanese such a success, and to show how
Japan´s experience relates to the U.S., this book
gives an overview of the Japanese economy and
culture. The Japanese-American relationship is
presented, with its problems and its importance.
Then the Japanese themselves are described in
terms of their ability to cope with modern
problems. Japanese business is traced, and
society at large is described. Informal
assessments of the culture and the success of
Japan are included.

173. Gibney, Frank. Miracle by Design: The Real
Reasons Behind Japan´s Economic Success. New
York: Times Books, 1982.

Written from the perspective of an American who
lived and made a living in Japan, this work´s aim
is to acquaint Americans with the nature of
Japanese society and business. It explores the
internal composition of the Japanese business
community in the context of its political, social,
historical and economic foundations, seeking to
explain how their banks, companies, and
bureaucracy work and why union members consider
themselves to be part of management. It points
out the strong influence of American theories and
practices on Japanese management and business.
Work ethics, management and human capital, the
integrity of the company, and doing business in
Japan are also discussed. A future problem facing
the Japanese is its failure to combine
international business success with a sense of
international political, economic, and social
responsibility.

174. Gilder, George. "A Supply-Side Economics of the

Left." Public Interest. 72 (Summer 1983): 29-
43.

In the last 5 years, there has been a major shift
in the debate over U.S. economic policy. The
conservative microtheory, emphasizing incentives
and distortions of the economy by government
policy, has set the terms ofthe debate. Reich´s
The Next American Frontier and Minding
America´s Business have provided Liberals with a
systematic theory of government involvement in
social and industrial policy making. Reich
assumes the U.S. economy if fundamentally awry,
businesses are continuing to lose ground, and
progress in advanced technologies is moving
slowly. Also he believes hostility between
business and government is preventing productivity
gains which have occurred in Europe and Asia. The
author believes Reich´s biggest misconception is
that growth stems from big business. Actually in
the last 2 years, entrepreneurship reached new
levels in business starts and venture capital
investments. Apart from Japan, the U.S. leads in
the creativity and productivity of its system.

175. Gresser, Julian. Partners in Prosperity:
     Strategic Industries for the United States and
     Japan. New York: McGraw-Hill Book Co., 1984.

     This text offers an exploration of two central
     tenets of industrial policy: one is that there can
     be a "trigger" mechanism whereby particular
     favored industries are picked by government and
     stimulated so that they will generate growth
     throughout the economy. A second is that
     negotiation is the method by which a free market
     can be approximated while at the same time
     strategic industries can be fostered. There is a
     historical survey of strategic industries, from
     British textiles to American railroads, etc. The
     Japanese model of accelerated development is then
     traced. The need for government action in
     triggering the strategic industries´ growth is
     then examined in case histories. The trade
     relationship between the U.S. and Japan is traced,
     showing that there have been several conflict
     periods of significance. A charter for a new
     U.S.-Japan partnership is then offered.

176. Guillain, Robert. The Japanese Challenge. Trans.
     Patrick O´Brian. Philadelphia: J.B. Lippincott
     Co., 1970.

     This book assesses the role of Japan as a world
     economic power. It offers some of the immediacy
     of a travel log. General descriptions of the

growth of Japan and the management-labor system
are given. The diplomatic status of Japan, as a
country without military power but dependent on
trade is examined. The relations of Japan and the
rest of the Asian Pacific countries are outlined.
Some discussion of the problems that the past has
bequeathed present-day Japan is offered, with a
treatment of various prospects for the future.

177. Hadley, Eleanor M. Japan's Export Competitiveness
in Third World Markets. Significant Issues Series
3, no. 2. Washington, D.C.: U.S. Export
Competitiveness Project, Center for Strategic and
International Studies, Georgetown University,
1981.

Written at the direction of the U.S. General
Accounting Office, this report is a comprehensive
analysis of U.S. and Japanese trading practices
and policies. Although noting the existence of
problems in certain areas, the study concludes
that the real problem lies in fundamental economic
factors such as relative rates of savings and
investment in the two countries, the time horizon
used for business judgments, the effort expended
to adapt products to specific export markets, and
the tendency for the Japanese to concentrate their
export efforts on products that have the largest
export potential. The same factors that impede
the U.S. effort to compete effectively with Japan
bilaterally are seen to impact on the U.S.'s
performance with relation to the Third World
markets. The issue of Japan's industrial policy
is also treated.

178. Hamilton, A. "Japan's New Game." Management
Today. (March 1984): 76-79,150.

Japan's new prime minister, Yasuhiro Nakasone, is
viewed by American and Europeans as possibly
promoting better trade policies, reducing
protectionism, and increasing Japan's defenses.
However, those in Japan see a number of internal
problems that need to be faced. The country may
be reaching a market saturation point. Some
exports have dropped for the first time since the
war. Japan's coordinated industrial policies may
not work so well with the new technology.
Japanese policies may move toward a more workable
relationship with the U.S. Japan also has a
growing national debt and a better relation with
the U.S. might help with these money problems.

179. Harper, E. L. "Does America Need an Industrial
Policy?" American Chamber of Commerce in Japan
Journal. 20.10 (Oct. 1983): 9-13.

The economic and industrial development of the
U.S. is described along with policy measures
needed for economic growth. A presentation of the
meaning of an industrial policy and the role it
plays in industrial development is provided, as
well as public and private attitudes. The
accomplishments of Japan's industrial policy are
reviewed.

180. Heenan, David A. "Building Industrial Cooperation
Through Japanese Strategies." Business Horizons.
28.6 (Nov./Dec. 1985): 9-14.

This paper argues for basic changes in U.S.
antitrust laws and enforcement as a step in
improving U.S. international competitiveness.
Japan's success in foreign markets arises from its
coordinated industrial policies. Asian and
European countries are following Japan's example.
In these countries, corporate size is viewed as
increasing competition on the world markets. The
U.S., however, for the past 70 years, has viewed
cartelization as a hindrance to competition. This
has left the U.S. in a disadvantageous position
internationally. Creating a national industrial
policy based on Japanese strategies means changing
antitrust practices. A good starting place is
with the advanced technology industries. The U.S.
semiconductor field is already headed in this
direction, combining free entreprise with
industrial cooperation.

181. Heenan, David A. "A Split-Level Approach to
National Industrial Policy." New Managment. 1.3
(1984): 34-38.

The debate over a national industrial policy is
divided along party lines. The Reagan
Administration seeks to reduce the government's
involvement in the economy, while the Democrats
believe in pursuing governmental aid to industry
similar to Japan. A survey of 1,500 chief
executives and other managers reveals a majority
preference for the current regulated free
enterprise system. A new ideology may evolve
combining market oriented economics with a
collaborative economic organization. This split-
level approach to a national industrial policy
would preserve free enterprise and economic
regulations. By modifying and replacing
regulations with new ones aimed at promoting
economic growth, new competitive forces will be
released in the marketplace. The split-level
approach would enhance cooperation between
government, business, and labor in the policy
making process. With this approach, joint

ventures such as Semiconductor Research
Cooperative and the Microelectronics and Computer
Cooperative would be greatly benefitted.

182. Higashi, Chikara. Japanese Trade Policy
Formulation. New York: Praeger, 1983.

This book is written with the intention of
dispelling some myths regarding Japanese trade
policy formation. Often Japan has been the
scapegoat for U.S. difficulties, and while
appreciating how this has happened, the author
attempts to correct this misapprehension. In
order to do this, there is a clarification of the
institutions which Japan uses to accomplish its
trade policy formation. Then there are studies of
conflict case studies, in which U.S. and Japanese
interests have clashed: steel, automobiles,
agricultural products, telecommunications, and
policy coordination. Conflicts which took place
from 1977 and 1981 are studied, with information
gathered in Tokyo and in Washington. The reasons
for each conflict are explored, and the handling
of each is outlined through domestic political
maneuverings and negotiations between the
countries. Included are the viewpoints of the
economists, the political scientists, and the
behavioral scientists who have written on the
conflict process, thereby offering a balanced and
perspicatious set of conclusions.

183. Hiraoka, L. S. "U.S-Japanese Competition in High-
Technology Fields." Technological Forecasting &
Social Change. 26.1 (Aug. 1984): 1-10.

This article contrasts the difference in the
economic systems between the U.S. and Japan in
high-tech development and marketing. The U.S.
leaves innovation to the private sector, while
Japan advances result from both the private sector
and the MITI's promotion of an industrial policy.
A new group, the Semiconductor Research Corp., is
advocating reciprocal trade legislation which
would match Japan's protectionist measures. The
outcome of the U.S.-Japan competitive struggle
over high-tech markets will be determined by the
technical and commercial skills of the private
sector. Statistics are given for 1966-81.

184. Hollerman, Leon, ed. Japan and the United States:
Economic and Political Adversaries. Boulder, Co.:
Westview Press, 1980.

The essays in this book are designed to contribute
to the economic and trade debates between the
United States and Japan. Contributions are given

by both American and Japanese writers. Besides
the evolution and future of U.S.-Japanese trade
relations, topics include U.S.-Japanese relations
in science and technology, locomotive strategy and
U.S. protectionism, and Japanese technological
superiority. ASEAN and its relations with Japan
and the U.S. are also discussed.

185. Holmes, Peter A. "Sparks Fly Over Industrial
Policy." Nation's Business. 71.11 (Nov. 1983):
22-24.

In U.S. government circles the issue of an
industrial policy is causing a great debate. The
American Federation of Labor-Congress of
Industrial Organizations (AFL-CIO) support the
idea, including the creation of a National
Industrial Policy Board. This board would be
composed of labor, business, and government
representatives. Liberal Democrats are also
strong supporters of the plan. The success of
Japan's centralized planning, coordinated by
business and government policy makers, has greatly
influenced the debate. President Reagan's
Commission on Industrial Competition may represent
a conservative alternative to improving long-term
growth and competitive in basic and high-tech
industries.

186. "Industrial Policy: Is It the Answer?" Business
Week (Industrial Edition). 2797 (4 July 1983):
54-62.

The debate over a U.S. national industrial policy
has various schools of thought. These include 1)
accelerationists, 2) adjusters, 3) targeters, 4)
central planners, and 5) bankers. Critics of an
industrial policy argue that it would slow
industrial growth and be subject to bureaucratic
manipulation. They argue there is a lack of
evidence to show that foreign subsidies are
responsible for declining U.S. industries and that
the government could adequately identify "sunrise"
industries. The marketplace should be left alone
to bring recovery. Advocates reply that the
government has been involved in industrial policy
making for a long time, that it is not difficult
to spot sunrise industries, and that the cost for
not having an industrial policy is further decline
and loss of competitive power. An industrial
policy could detect changes in the market, thereby
preventing political bailouts. Time, effort, and
money would be saved increasing human welfare.

187. "An Industry Plea for the Freedom to Compete."
Business Week (Industrial Edition). 2793 (June 6,

1983): 59-60.

The idea of a U.S. industrial policy is becoming
more popular. Many Americans see foreign
competitors, especially Japan, benefitting from
U.S. science and technology at their expense. The
National Research Council and the Business-Higher
Education Forum have asked the Reagan
Administration to create policies to aid business
in bringing new products to market. The
government should create an institutional
framework to assist industrial productivity and
competitiveness based on research universities,
industrial technology, venture capital, and a
favorable entrepreneurial environment. The
government first must improve incentives for
technological growth through tax reform, research
and development, patents, antitrust, and trade.

188. "Industry's Top Execs Out on a Limb." Iron Age.
     227.1 (2 Jan. 1984): 62-94.

U.S. industrial executives discuss common economic
problems: the state of the economy, international
competition, technological innovation, and
corporate survival strategies. Lee Iacocca,
Chrysler Corp., believes the coming year will be
primarily concerned with the question of
industrial policy. Temporary restraints against
Japan may be needed. John F. Welch, General
Electric, seeks "quality recovery" based on
investments yielding long-term gains in
productivity and real income. The old industrial
management policies of the past have failed and
should not be repeated. The farming industry is
discussed and its recovery is seen to depend on
sustained international economic growth, a lower
dollar exchange rate, and government policies
aimed at making U.S. products more competitive in
foreign markets. Shipbuilding, steel, machine
tools, and railcars are other industries
discussed.

189. Japan Economic Institute of America. Japan's
     Industrial Policies: What Are They, Do They
     Matter, and Are They Different from Those in the
     United States? Washington, D.C.: Japan Economic
     Institute of America, 1984.

The picture of Japanese government intervention in
economics is exaggerated, because the current
situation shows that government is growing less
influential. The credit that has often been given
to Japan's government for postwar growth is also
out of proportion, because there have been many
factors contributing to that growth.

Macroeconomic policies were more important than
microeconomic policies, except that the use of
protection from imports was significant. Some
industries received special financing from the
government, but not only new industries received
this support, as is sometimes thought. Data shows
that successes in Japanese industries cannot be
attributed solely to government support, and the
overall comparison between the Japanese industrial
policy and the American indicates that the two are
not very far apart. Extensive data is examined in
relation to the role of government financing in
supporting growth.

190. Japan-United States Economic Relations Group.
     Appendix to the Report of the Japan-United States
     Economic Relations Group. Washington, D.C.:
     Japan-United States Economic Relations Group,
     1981.

     This is a collection of background studies on
     U.S.-Japanese economic relations used in preparing
     the Report. An analysis of cyclical and marco-
     structural issues is presented covering an
     historical overview from the late 1960´s,
     interdependence, and coordination of macroeconomic
     policy. Additional topics include energy, the
     decline of U.S. productivity growth, the
     liberalization of Japan´s foreign trade and
     foreign exchange transactions, legal protectionism
     in the U.S., issues involving political conflict,
     and Japanese investment in the U.S.

191. Japan-United States Economic Relations Group.
     Report of the Japan-United States Economic
     Relations Group: Prepared for the President of the
     United States and the Prime Minister of Japan.
     Washington, D.C.: Japan-United States Economic
     Relations Group, 1981.

     A broad range of bilateral and multilateral issues
     are examined relating to U.S.-Japan economic
     relations. While a general healthy economic and
     political relation exists between the two
     countries, there are however a number of problems
     that need to be faced into order to more
     effectively address global challenges. These
     problems consist of inadequate consultative
     mechanisms between the two governments, false or
     outdated perceptions of the other country, poor
     U.S. economic performance, lagging liberalization
     of Japanese markets, and a failure for both
     governments and private sectors to face up to
     difficult problems. The study begins by providing
     an overview of the global U.S.-Japan economic
     relationship, and then proceeds to examine

individual issues involving both countries.

192. Japan-United States Economic Relations Group.
     Supplemental Report of the Japan-United States
     Economic Relations Group: Prepared for the
     President of the United States and the Prime
     Minister of Japan. Washington, D.C.: Japan-United
     States Economic Relations Group, 1981.

     This supplementary report discusses the need for
     international economic leadership, U.S. and
     Japanese trade policies, potential bilateral
     economic issues, energy, and a move toward a
     comprehensive partnership.

193. Johnson, Chalmers A., ed. The Industrial Policy
     Debate. San Francisco, Calif.: Institute for
     Contemporary Studies Press, 1984.

     These 11 essays and summary chapters consider the
     recent proposals by Democrats and others seeking a
     national industrial policy to counteract the
     structural deterioration of the U.S. economy. The
     first six essays focus on the nature of the
     proposed industrial policy, tracing their roots to
     Japanese and European government acts, on the
     problems of implementation, and on the evidence
     regarding industrial decline. The last five
     essays explore for specific aspects of industrial
     policy: innovation, trade policy, banking and
     financial regulations, national defense
     implications, and tax reform. For the most part,
     these assessments and consequences of an
     industrial policy are written with conservative,
     supply-side economics, or Republican viewpoints.

194. Jones, T. M., et al. "Industrial Policy:
     Influencing the International Marketplace."
     Journal of Contemporary Business. 11.1 (1982):
     1-148.

     Eleven contributions by T.M. Jones, R. Holland, W.
     Eberle, I. Magaziner, P. Tiffany, J. Calton, J.
     Johansson, S. Cohen, Tran Van Tho, T. Roehl, and
     others are given on various aspects of U.S.
     industrial policy. Topics include the political
     implications of the 1980´s, the development of a
     strategy of less market interference, the need of
     a national consensus for economic rejuvenation,
     and the problem of the declining steel industry.
     An historical review of industrial policy
     developments in the world auto industry,
     particularly Europe and Japan is given. In
     addition, examples of the Swedish, French, and
     Japanese economic models are discussed, along with
     the Japanese textile industry experience.

Industrial policy in developing countries is also reviewed.

195. Kantrow, Alan M. "The Political Realities of Industrial Policy." Harvard Business Review. 61.5 (Sept./Oct. 1983): 76-86.

There is general public awareness that the condition of industrial and international competition have fundamentally changed. Should the U.S. create an industrial policy and the institutional apparatus to implement it, or should free market forces be allowed to work to regain industrial competiveness on the international markets? A round table of experts gathered to discuss the government's role in bringing about an industrial recovery. George Eads, University of Maryland, warns the Japanese more fully utilize high technology than the U.S. by moving beyond just electronics to applications in all industries. Lester Thurow, Massachusetts Institute of Technology, says Japan has benefited because its people are more willing to accept major economic change.

196. Kikuchi, Makoto. Japanese Electronics: A Worm's-Eye View of Its Evolution. Trans. Simul International. Tokyo: The Simul Press, Inc., 1983.

This book offers a narrative depiction of Japan's success. There is a treatment of how the world views Japan, and how Japan learned to compete successfully. The key use of technology in Japan is contrasted with the way the U.S. economic system is operating. Some attention is given to questioning what the new age will bring in technology and changes in culture.

197. Kimura, Shigeru. Japan's Science Edge: How the Cult of Anti-Science Thought in America Limits U.S. Scientific and Technological Progress. Lanham, Md.: University Press of America, 1975.

This book offers a critique of the social attitudes in the U.S. in recent years. The "counter culture" and ecology movements are interpreted as anti-science, and as hampering the U.S. in its competitiveness in the world economy. The Nixon years showed a growing disinterest in technological progress, and Reagan's space program also demonstrates a lag in scientific concern as compared with Japan. The influential writers in the U.S. who have caused a slowdown in the technology race are identified and discussed.

198. Kotabe, Masaaki. "The Roles of Japanese
     Industrial Policy for Export Success: A
     Theoretical Perspective." Columbia Journal of
     World Business. 20.3 (Fall 1985): 59-64.

     An examination of the theoretical background to
     Japan's industrial policy is provided, with the
     consideration of several theories. There has been
     increased interest in the Japanese experience on
     the part of the U.S. in recent years, due to some
     structural problems the U.S. economy is
     developing. There are advocates of more strategy
     for the U.S. in its economic development. And
     there is a rationale for any country to wish to
     assert its strength along the lines of a trading
     posture that will enhance its exports and give it
     a positive balance of trade worldwide. But in
     order to enable the U.S. to use some of the
     Japanese methods, there would need to be more
     cooperation between policy-makers and the
     corporate decision-makers. Otherwise it would be
     difficult to bring into being any genuine changes
     in industrial policy.

199. Krugman, Paul R. Brookings Papers on Economic
     Activity. 1 (1984): 77-121.

     The issue addressed is the question of whether
     industrial policies in other countries,
     particularly Japan, are a major contributor to
     American economic problems. These foreign
     industrial policies could be hurting the U.S.
     ecomony in three ways: 1) by the displacement of
     American workers from high to low wage sectors; 2)
     by "strategic" manipulation of the conditions of
     competition in oligopolistic industries; and 3) by
     using industrial targeting, which has resulted in
     excluding the U.S. from sectors yielding valuable
     external economies. Although each of these makes
     theoretical sense, they do not stand up under
     examination.

200. Lavoie, Don. "Two Varieties of Industrial Policy:
     A Critique." Cato Journal. 4.2 (Fall 1984): 457-
     484.

     This article concerns the U.S. industrial policy
     debate between Robert Reich and Felix Rohatyn.
     The similarities and differences between the two
     positions reveal a fundamental weakness in the
     concept of industrial policy itself. Following
     Japan's example, as advocated by Mr. Reich, would
     set up an organization similar to the MITI, and
     the author argues that this would be politically
     dangerous in the U.S.

201. LeCerf, Barry H., and Edwin W. Bowers. "America´s
     Labor Chief Talks About Jobs and the Jobless."
     Iron Age. 226.20 (July 22, 1983): 27-37.

     In an interview, Secretary of Labor Donovan said
     the forecasts dooming basic American industries
     are premature. These industries, particularly oil
     and steel, are experiencing structural
     adjustments, not decline, and they are necessary
     for defense purposes. He further adds that
     structural unemployment is a natural part of the
     economy, the service sector is growing
     dramatically, and industry and labor can play an
     important role in retraining workers. The
     enterprise zone is Donovan´s conception of an
     industrial policy, more an incentive plan than an
     actual policy. The government should stay out of
     collective bargaining. The Japanese are making
     Americans aware of better cooperation on the plant
     floor.

202. McClenahen, John S. "How Trade Rules Tie Our
     Hands." Industry Week. 206.5 (Sept. 1, 1980):
     34-40.

     Since 1975, the U.S. has had annual balance of
     payment deficits. Foreign governments are
     subsidizing their exports and protecting their
     markets making it difficult for the U.S. to
     compete. American executives believe the
     government actually works against industry on
     export issues. From 1947 to 1979, the U.S. share
     of the world´s exports has dropped from 50% to
     13%. The U.S. faces tough competition in the
     1980´s from the EEC, Japan, and the Third World.
     U.S. export policy must be rewritten and the U.S.
     needs a national industrial policy to deal with
     the national and international issues.

203. McCraw, Thomas K., ed. America versus Japan: A
     Comparative Study of Business-Government Relations
     Conducted at the Harvard Business School. Boston,
     Mass.: Harvard Business School Press, 1986.

     This comparative study centers on the public
     policies that have evolved between business and
     government interaction in the U.S. and Japan.
     Composed of a collection of in-depth essays
     written by leading U.S. researchers, the book
     focuses on nine major areas including trade,
     investment, production and distribution,
     agriculture, energy, the environment, financial
     institutions, taxes, and investment. No single
     explanation is given for national differences in
     government policies toward business, but rather an
     interplay of geographic, political, historical,

and cultural forces. The emerging of differing
economic goals and decision-making methods has
brought these two nations, once closely
cooperating, gradually into a pattern of conflict
over trade and capital mobility.

204. McCulloch, R. "Trade Deficits, Industrial
Competitiveness, and the Japanese." California
Management Review. 27.2 (Winter 1985): 140-161.

The imbalance of trade between the U.S. and its
major trading partners, especially Japan, has
created a demand for policies designed to increase
the international competitiveness of American
industries. Since the U.S. trade deficit is a
result of domestic and international macroeconomic
conditions, there will be little effect by
policies designed to promote the competitiveness
of individual industries. A national industrial
policy is needed to rectify the situation.

205. McKenna, Regis, et al. "Industrial Policy and
International Competition in High Technology."
California Management Review. 26.2 (Winter
1984): 15-32.

Capital formation by U.S. high-tech firms has been
hindered by Japanese competitive strategies. The
Japanese government has protected their high-tech
firms making available cheaper sources of capital
for productive investment than the corresponding
U.S. firms. By acquiring foreign technology
through licensing agreements, Japanese companies
have freed capital from research and development
for innovative high-quality, low-cost products.
Further the Japanese government has protected its
domestic markets from U.S. competition. In order
to make U.S. high-tech firms more competitive, it
will be necessary to formulate an industrial
policy for productive investments by providing tax
credits for R & D expenditures. Technology
licensing agreements with Japan must be tied to
U.S. accessibility to Japan's domestic markets.

206. Modic, Stanley J. "A U.S. Industrial Policy? Yes
- No." Industry Week. 219.4 (14 Nov. 1983): 38-
44.

The recession, rapid technological change, and
international competition have given rise to the
question of a national industrial policy for the
U.S. The meaning of an industrial policy can
range from an "aggregate law of the micropolicies"
to explicit government economic intervention.
Robert B. Reich, author of _The Next American
Frontier_, sees a national industrial policy

facilitating strategic planning between labor,
business, and government. The government role
should center on retraining, promoting research
and development efforts, establishing conditional
protectionist measures, and coordinating
government programs with the private sector.
Jerry Jasinowski, economist for the National
Association of Manuacturers, argues otherwise.
The real cause of industrial decay resides in high
interest rates, high levels of the federal
deficit, and the overvalued dollar. The
government needs to direct its efforts at these
instead of creating a national industrial policy.

207. Morley, James William, ed. Prologue to the
     Future: The United States and Japan in the
     Postindustrial Age. Lexington, Mass.: Lexington
     Books, D.C. Heath & Co., 1974.

     Both the U.S. and Japan, as advanced societies,
     face the problems and promises of the new era in
     which high technology, affluence, education and
     urbanization are important features. Older
     loyalties continue to attract large segments of
     the populations, and frictions of the past remain.
     Increases in the service sector and the
     information revolution may bring both countries
     closer to a convergence and to postindustrial
     society. Future prospects from writers from the
     U.S. and Japan are offered, on topics such as the
     economy, the polity, and the city.

208. Murrin, Thomas J. "American Strategies for
     Productivity and Profitability - A Consensus Based
     Policy Formation Mechanism." Vital Speeches of
     the Day. 49.4 (1 Dec. 1982): 124-128.

     The U.S. is on the edge of a major economic
     crisis, produced by low capital investment, too
     little spending on R&D, high labor demands, and
     little attention to improving productivity and
     product quality. Federal laws and regulations
     have encourage this situation. As an industrial
     policy this has been disastrous. The Japanese
     targeting policies in the areas of micro-
     electronics, computers, communications, machine
     tools, and robots have directly challenged U.S.
     competitive potentials. The fight for industrial
     supremacy is founded on these advanced
     technologies and the U.S. needs to rectify its
     position rapidly. Six strategies are offered for
     improving performance: 1) improving motivation and
     management techniques, 2) increasing office and
     factory automation, 3) improving quality, 4)
     increased application of value analysis
     techniques, 5) better utilization of resources,

and 6) strategically locating new factories.

209. Naylor, P. "Bringing Home the Lessons of Japanese
     Management." Personnel Management. (March 1984):
     34-37.

     American personnel director toured Japan to study
     management practices, labor relations, and
     industrial policies. The applicability of these
     practices and policies to Western oranizations is
     examined. On the whole, there are major
     differences between Japanese and American decision
     making processes. Japanese managers have a well-
     rounded career development which provides them
     with many career opportunities.

210. Neef, M. G. "An Industrial Policy: What Does It
     Mean?" Business Horizons. 27.6 (Nov./Dec.
     1984): 43-49.

     There are different views on the direction a U.S.
     national industrial policy should take. The
     Japanese model of industrial policy is often
     cited, while others suggest a variety of programs
     from tax incentives to government support for
     emerging industries. However, the basic shift
     from an manufacturing to a service-oriented
     economy is often overlooked. Changing political
     parties and a tendency to add to existing programs
     results in producing only piece-meal solutions.

211. "No: Let the Market Work." Business Week. 2797
     (July 4, 1983): 57+.

     It is believed by many economists that a national
     industrial policy would be harmful to the U.S.
     Japan's centralized planning has not played as an
     important a role in their economic success as is
     currently thought. Economic changes should be
     made by adjustments in the marketplace. A policy
     governmentally imposed onto the economy would be
     destructive.

212. Ohmae, Kenichi. Triad Power: The Coming Shape of
     Global Competition. New York: Free Press, 1985.

     Western executives have a false impression about
     the competitiveness of Japanese companies. This
     is on account of the high visibility of their
     exports - cars, consumer electronics, cameras,
     watches, etc. This has led them to concentrate on
     labor relations and quality circles at the expense
     of competitive strategy, R&D, and profitability.
     Examples are given of U.S. markets in which the
     Japanese have done poorly. In order for Western
     companies to regain their competitive strength,

they need only to take a different approach to
international strategy. Companies will survive
which concentrate their efforts on winning market
shares and sales volume in the Triad, the markets
of Europe, the U.S., and Japan. The third world
only offers peripheral opportunities. Global
competitors must penetrate all three markets
simultaneously with new products, seeking
distribution or cooperative ventures with other
companies in the Triad. Case studies are
presented of successful strategies by Triad
companies.

213. Ozawa, Terutomo. Japan's Technological Challenge
to the West, 1950-1974: Motivation and
Accomplishment. Cambridge, Mass.: MIT Press,
1974.

Technology has been a crucial factor in Japan's
recent productivity and economic growth. The
postwar technological environment of Japan is
described. The technological relationships with
the U.S. and other Asian countries are examined,
and the incentives and opportunities for Japanese
technological progress are identified. The goal
of catching up with the West and the assimilation
of Western technologies seem to be the basis for
Japan's success. Methods by which Japan imported
and adapted technology are explored.
International monetary and energy crises are
shocks which Japan has weathered.

214. Pepper, Thomas, et al. The Competition: Dealing
with Japan. New York: Praeger, 1985.

By 1990, Japan will become the second largest
economy. The authors, members of the Hudson
Institute, stress the need of U.S. companies and
government policymakers to recognize the threat of
Japanese firms and the opportunities of the
Japanese markets. Rather than calling for a
national economic strategy, they seek changes in
government attitudes and corporate action to
become more competitive. Chapters discuss Japan's
economy, industrial policies, financial system,
new and declining industries, and business and
policy implications. The Japanese economy is
changing because of natural economic evolution,
which has rendered the MITI strategy of developing
infant industries increasingly ineffective. The
growing complexity of the economy has reduced the
ability of the Japanese government to target
sectors, industries, or firms for specific
purposes. These economic forces have the
possibility of opening new opportunities for U.S.
exports, for the development of the service

sector, and for cooperation with Japanese
companies.

215. Pugel, Thomas A., and Robert G. Hawkins, eds.
     Fragile Interdependence: Economic Issues in U.S.-
     Japanese Trade and Investment. Lexington, Mass.:
     Lexington Books, D.C. Heath and Co., 1986.

     This collection of papers addresses economic
     issues that contribute to stress in U.S.-Japanese
     trade and investment. It intends to provide
     policy-oriented discussions of the important
     issues of market acess, international investment,
     and international technological competition.
     Other issues include trade restrictions and import
     policies, the internationalization and
     liberalization of Japanese financial markets, the
     increasing role of multinational corporations in
     both countries by the two-way flows of foreign
     direct investments, and the different industrial
     policies of each country.

216. Reich, Robert B. "Making Industrial Policy."
     Foreign Affairs. 60.4 (Spring 1982): 852-881.

     During the 1970's, the advanced industrial
     economies experienced slower growth rates and
     heightened international competition. In face of
     the threat to domestic industries from imports,
     the traditional response has been to call for
     greater tariff protection. However a distinction
     should be made between slow and rapid adjustments.
     Slow adjustments are much more difficult to
     contend with and a managed adjustment procedure is
     a better method of response. Managed adjustment
     can be achieved by a nation by entering an
     explicit bargaining relationship between
     government, business, and labor in which
     adjustment is the common objective. The
     government needs to formulate an industrial policy
     activated by means of contracts in which its aid
     is exchanged for mutually agreed shifts in the
     private sector resources. Declining industries
     and their dependents would be fully compensated
     for the economic hardships brought about by the
     shifting economic environment. To accomplish
     this, the U.S. needs to become better equipped in
     acquiring strategic business information,
     negotiating adjustment agreements, and
     coordinating policies. This requires the creation
     of new political institutions to handle the new
     economic realities.

217. Reich, Robert B. "What Kind of Industrial
     Policy?." Journal of Business Strategy. 5.1
     (Summer 1984): 10-17.

Industrial development in the U.S. appears as a patchwork policy when one analyzes industries receiving benefits from tax breaks, research funding, and subsidized loans. By contrast, Japan coordinates its tax, loans, patents, and education policies into a successful industrial policy. The U.S. needs to make its macroeconomic intervention more consistent with macroeconomic objectives. International competition is forcing the U.S. to develop a closer link between government and business by means of a centralized industrial policy. Two tables are given listing paid corporate income tax by industry and industries receiving research funding.

218. Richardson, Bradley M., and Taizo Veda, eds. Business and Society in Japan: Fundamentals for Businessmen. New York: Praeger, 1981.

This book was produced jointly by the Honda Motor Company and Ohio State Unversity, in an effort to provide more information about Japan for American businessmen. It offers a comprehensive overview of Japanese economics: business and labor´s relations are summarized; the growth and competitiveness of the economic system are underscored; the political environment of Japanese business is sketched, trade relationships are discussed; and the experience of modernization is summarized. The authors consist of a multidisciplinary team, including economists, and specialists in law, education, business, the media, sociology, political science, and history. They challenge some of the myths which have grown up in America about Japan, hoping to explain Japan´s success and note the sometimes negative consequences of that success.

219. Richmond, Frederick W., and Michael Kahan. How to Beat the Japanese at Their Own Game. Englewood Cliffs, N.J.: Prentice-Hall, 1983.

Written by a U. S. Congressman, this book is a general narrative about the U. S.-Japanese business situation. There are references to testimony given at the hearings of the Joint Economic Committee on US-Japan Trade Relations in an anecdotal fashion. There is an emphasis on the U.S.´s export situation, and the desire to increase those exports. The book treats the economics and statistics of the U.S.-Japanese relationship in a cursory way.

220. Roehl, T. W. "Industrial Policy and Trade: Three Myths of Japan." Journal of Contemporary Business. 11.1 (June 1982): 129-138.

The United States has begun to study more closely
Japan's industrial policy experiences, especially
its relationship to foreign trade. There are
however three myths about Japan's policies that
must be dispelled: 1) that the Ministry of
International Trade and Industry controls exports,
2) that Japanese companies use unfair pricing
strategies to capture foreign markets, and 3) that
Japan's general trading companies are the key to
its success in international markets. These myths
are discussed in detail.

221. Roemer, John E. U.S.-Japanese Competition in
International Markets: A Study of the Trade-
Investment Cycle in Modern Capitalism. Berkeley,
Calif.: Institute of International Studies,
University of California, 1975.

Taking the view that Japan's rise to hegemony is a
central event in modern political economy, this
book discusses international competition as a key
to the development of capitalism. Japan's
competitive status is viewed in this historical
context. International trade and investment in
manufactures are studied. The four stages through
which a country grows as an international
competitor are identified and Japan is related to
the stages, along with other nations. The export
of capital in labor intensive industries is
discussed. New international relationships are
forecast.

222. Rowen, Hobart. "Prosperity, Growth, and Quality:
The Threat from Protectionist Policies." Quality
Progress. 19.2 (Feb. 1986): 18-21.

Free trade is losing a number of adherents in
governments around the world. Reasons for this
occurrence include: rising problems of debts and
exchange rates, increasing tensions in
international trade, coupled with growing
protectionist measures and trade restrictions, and
the continuing trade controversy between the U.S.
and Japan. The success of Japanese firms can be
contributed to closely tracing consumer demand and
to quality control. This is supplemented by good
basic education programs and the importation of
technology and ideas. The U.S. should respond to
its trade imbalance by changing its macroeconomic
policies to deal with reducing its deficit,
correcting the overvaluation of the dollar, and
expanding foreign markets. There should also be
instituted a more rational economic planning
system incorporating government, business, and
labor efforts. Further the quality of business

management should be improved.

223. Schlossstein, Steven. Trade War: Greed, Power,
     and Industrial Policy on Opposite Sides of the
     Pacific. New York: Congdon & Weed (Distributed by
     St. Martin's Press), 1984.

     The author recommends the acceptance of a U.S.
     industrial policy. This policy for
     reindustrialization should use a strategy and
     tactics appropriate to improving the U.S. trade
     position and widen American comparative advantage.
     This means a move away from a concentration on
     "fast food and ICBM's" toward brain-trust
     selected, nonservice manufacturing areas. He
     praises the Japanese for concentrating on
     production and quality, and critizes American
     industry for its short-term profit orientation and
     for its financial mergers.

224. Schultze, Charles L. "Industrial Policy: A
     Dissent." Brookings Review. 2.1 (Fall 1983): 3-
     12.

     Recent recessions and slow productivity growth
     have resulted in two competing doctrines to
     address these economic problems. Proponents of an
     industrial policy assume that the U.S. has been
     "de-industrializing," while other economies,
     especially Japan have successfully maintained
     industrial growth through a business-government
     coordinated industrial policy. The author
     contends that the U.S. does not need such an
     industrial policy where the federal government
     would have an major role in shaping the allocation
     of resources to firms and industries. Supply-side
     economics proposes an alternative. Changes in
     fiscal and monetary policies could promote
     industrial development and economic growth.
     Macroeconomic policies need to be formulated to
     create a favorable environment for business
     expansion. This involves making some difficult
     choices regarding national objectives. Further,
     there are structural problems which still need
     workable solutions.

225. Schultze, Charles L. "Industrial Policy: A
     Solution in Search of a Problem." California
     Management Review. 25.4 (Summer 1983): 5-15.

     The author argues that the reasons for an
     industrial policy in the U.S. are unfounded. The
     deindustrialization of the U.S. is their major
     assumption for advocating a policy protecting
     declining industries and promoting new ones.
     There is no empirical basis for this. In the

1970's, U.S. industrial performance was equal to
or better than other industrial economies. U.S.
employment increased 26%, while Japan's grow only
by 8%. Only Japan and Italy excelled the U.S. in
increased manufacturing production. The U.S. fell
behind in basic metals and automobile industries,
but this arose from structural difficulties in
these industries. It is doubtful the U.S.
government could adequately formulate criteria for
selecting successful industries. Although Japan's
economic success is attributed to its industrial
policy, it really lies in the Japanese culture and
economy.

226. Scott, B. R. "National Strategy for Stonger U.S.
     Competitiveness." Harvard Business Review. 62.2
     (March/April 1984): 77-91.

The last 15 years has seen the U.S. slip in its
portion of the world GNP and suffer unfavorable
balance of trade. In comparison with our major
Asian competitors, we need a major reevaluation of
our economic policies and a new look at the theory
of comparative advantage. This 200 year old
theory is essentially static and fails to describe
the current world accurately. The Japanese have
shown that comparative advantage can still be
applicable if its dynamic nature is managed and
used constructively. The U.S. needs to recognize
this in order to remain internationally
competitive. This requires a national economic
strategy of a broad perspective.

227. Sobel, Robert. IBM vs. Japan: The Struggle for
     the Future. New York: Stein and Day, 1986.

In a cursory and sometimes polemical work, this
author argues that the Japanese computer industry
offers no real challenge to IBM, since there is
not enough creativity and flexibility in the
Japanese industry. The account relies on the view
that the advances made in Japan have been the
result of borrowed technology.

228. Solo, Robert. "Industrial Policy." Journal of
     Economic Issues. 18.3 (Sept. 1984): 697-714.

Anti-trust policy in the United States is reviewed
from 1890 to 1940. The effects of anti-trust laws
on industrial performance has been overlooked by
the legal community. Anti-trust policies have had
the effect of punishing successful companies, and
consequently the U.S. has lost its industrial
leadership. Greater cooperation is recommended
between the public and private sectors. Italian
and Japanese industrial policies are offered as

models.

229. Srodes, J. L. "Idea´s Time Comes - and Comes
     Again." Financial Planning. 13.7 (July 1984):
     25-26.

     The issue of a national industrial policy for the
     U.S. is discussed. An industrial policy
     coordinating government intervention may be better
     than sporadic ad hoc policies. Examples of
     successful ad hoc government interventions to aid
     companies are given: Penn Central Railroad,
     Amtrak, Lockheed, and Chrysler Corporation.
     Although an industrial policy would liken the U.S.
     with its chief competitors, West Germany and
     Japan, it is believed the U.S. would not benefit
     from one. U.S. industrial productivity is
     superior to its foreign competitors.

230. Striner, Herbert E. Regaining the Lead: Policies
     for Economic Growth. New York: Praeger, 1984.

     Putting aside the major economic theories, this
     book begins with the view that economics has not
     been able to explain reality. The chief problem
     is that none accounts for the poor performance of
     the U.S. in the last few decades in relation to
     its competitors. The positions of Germany and
     Japan are described in the political-economic
     order. A new model of capitalism, called "shared
     capitalism" is then presented, in which instincts
     for cooperation come to the fore, in the place of
     the old "laissez-faire" system. The conclusion is
     offered that the U.S. can take control of its
     economy and regain its strong position in the
     world economic order.

231. "Survey Sees Intensifying Japan, U.S.
     Competition." Japan Economic Journal. 23.1158
     (May 7, 1985): 8.

     The Japan Industrial Policy Research Institute
     released a study stating competition between
     Japanese and American firms will accelerate in the
     fields of information, communications, and
     transportation. The markets in these areas are
     expanding rapidly. Unlike manufacturing, the
     service industries are culturally and historically
     influenced. Consequently, more difficult problems
     may face U.S.-Japanese competition.

232. Tasca, Diane, ed. U.S.-Japanese Economic
     Relations: Cooperation, Competition, and
     Confrontation. Pergamon Policy Studies on U.S.
     and International Business. New York: Pergamon
     Press, Inc., 1980.

The U.S. and Japan have gone through periods of alternating cooperation and confrontation. Internal differences in ideologies, social structures, and values have contributed to this pattern, as have external factors which originate elsewhere in the international power scheme. Ambivalence in the power differential between the two countries makes for tension, as now there is no clear indication of which country is dominant. The present multipolar global power structure impacts on the relations between Japan and the U.S. Essays are presented on the measures which might best preserve the cooperative relationship that Japan and the U.S. have experienced since the war. Sources of conflict are identified.

233. Theobald, T. C. "Rediscovering America - The Free Marketplace." Vital Speeches of the Day. 50.14 (May 1, 1984): 429-432.

In a speech before the Financial Executive Institute, T. C. Theobald of Citibank applauds the values of the Midwest. Arguments for a national industrial policy are discussed. Recent criticism of American business acumen would have been better directed at governmental inconsistency. Japanese and U.S. productivity levels are analyzed. Japan leans toward protectionism and European governments are more intensely involved in business. The Japanese service industries have not become especially competitive with the help of governmental policies. The success rate in the U.S. for new firms is only 20%. There follows a discussion of the beliefs of the free market and the contradictory emotions relating to it.

234. Thurow, Lester C., ed. The Management Challenge: Japanese Views. Cambridge, Mass.: M.I.T. Press, 1985.

There is a selection of articles by Japanese academics and businessmen aimed at showing how they believe the competitive game is changing and the implications for U.S. and Japanese companies. A number of topics are covered: the gradual development of a sophisticated money market and bond financing in Japan; the potential long-term impact of the liberalization of the money market; an account of the way Japanese firms change and adapt through product diversification; a review of overseas expansion and the importance of short-term financial success; the government's industry policy and the competive dynamics of the Japanese economy; and the competitiveness of Japanese companies in the context of the declining influence of government as trade and capital laws deregulate Japan.

235. Thurow, Lester C. "Unsolicited Advice on Japanese American Economic Relations." Japan Economic Journal: International Weekly. 19.953 (May 5, 1981): 24-25.

In the form of an open letter to President Reagan, this article offers a plea for the restructuring and rebuilding of the U.S. economy after the pattern of the Japanese and German postwar reconstruction. This tactic is urged as a means of improving the U.S. competitive strength.

236. Tsurumi, Yoshi. "Japan's Challenge to the U.S.: Industrial Policies and Corporate Strategies." Columbia Journal of World Business. 17.2 (Summer 1982): 86-95.

The most important factor in shaping Japan's economic success is the complete reorganization which took place after the war. In this restructuring, the Japanese were able to borrow the best of the American system and the best of the German, taking managerial capitalism from the U.S. and financial capitalism from the Germans. This resulted in the new Japanese style of organization which can be characterized as "group capitalism." Careful planning in relation to the state of international markets and use of the latest technology available in various advanced countries characterizes this Japanese industrial policy. But it is the combination of fortunate circumstances for the Japanese that enhanced the profitability of the industries in Japan, rather than the industrial policies themselves that deserve the credit for Japan's success. The U.S. economy must begin to revitalize itself by taking corrective measures and restructuring. Trade barriers alone will not help to solve the imbalance between the U.S. and Japan.

237. United States. Congress. House of Representatives. Committee on Ways and Means. Subcommittee on Trade. Foreign Industrial Targeting and its Effects on U.S. Industries: Phase 1: Japan. Washington, D.C.: United States International Trade Commission, 1983.

These hearings were instituted at the U.S. International Trade Commission at the request of the Subcommittee on Trade. A definition of industrial targeting, its techniques and effects are presented. The relationship of targeting to U.S. legislation is explored. Japanese industrial policy is analyzed, with a historical overview, a description of the policy formation process, and a discussion of individual policies. There are discussions of specific industries.

238. United States. Congress. House of Representatives. Committee on Ways and Means. Subcommittee on Trade. High Technology and Japanese Industrial Policy: A Strategy for U.S. Policymakers. Prepared by Julian Gresser. Washington, D.C.: U. S. Government Printing Office, 1980.

Testimony was offered in response to a growing awareness of the seriousness of the U.S. bilateral trade deficits with Japan. It is shown that the Japanese semiconductor, computer and telecommunications industries are linked to its industrial future. Though competition from the Japanese was initially welcomed in the U.S., certain structural differences and policies in Japan caused a distortion of competitive forces. Existing trade remedies will not correct this distortion. A new perspective is offered. Measures that will not merely bloat the federal bureaucracy in the U.S. but meet the challenge offered by the corresponding Japanese policies are sought.

239. United States. Congress. Joint Economic Committee. International Competition in Advanced Industrial Sectors: Trade and Development in the Semi-Conductor Industry. Washngton, D. C.: U.S. Government Printing Office, 1982.

It is argued that the outcome of the international competition in electronics will have a great importance for the nation. Since the mid-1970´s, the semiconductor industry has developed rapidly, with Japan taking the lead. The U.S. has maintained success in responding to changing needs in the industry, while Japan has taken the lead in producing the standard products. The development of the American semiconductor industry is traced. Japan´s market power and government promotion in semiconductors is assessed. A comparison is made between the U.S. and Japan in their strategies for competing in electronics. The future prospects for that competition are assessed.

240. United States. Congress. Joint Economic Committee. Subcommittee on Economic Goals and Intergovernmental Policy. Foreign Industrial Targeting Policies: Hearing Before the Subcommittee on Economic Goals and Intergovernmental Policy of the Joint Economic Committee, Congress of the United States, Ninety-Eighth Congress, First Session, July 25, 1983..

Washington D.C.: U.S. Government Printing Office,
1984.

Three approaches to the targeting of economic
goals for particular industrial segments of the
U.S. economy are outlined. The emulative approach
is one which implies direct government involvement
in the selection of industries that would be
targeted and in the compensation of those
industries that would bear an undue share of the
burden of readjustment under the policy. This
approach would be similar to the methods used in
Japan. Another approach would be to close our
borders against imports from industries that we
have determined to be targeted by foreign
governments, but this would lead to economic
disaster. A third approach is a pure laissez-
faire one, in which the firms and individuals
would make the decisions, free from government
fiat. A middle ground approach is advocated in
the hearings.

241. United States. Congress. Joint Economic Committee.
     Subcommittee on Economic Goals and
     Intergovernmental Policy. Impact of Unfair
     Foreign Trade Practices: Hearing Before the
     Subcommittee on Economic Goals and
     Intergovernmental Policy of the Joint Economic
     Committee, Congress of the United States, Ninety-
     Ninth Congress, First Session, March 20, 1985.
     Washington, D.C.: U.S. Government Printing Office,
     1985.

     This hearing entertains testimony from
     representatives of U.S. industry regarding trade
     with Japan. Semiconductor industry and
     electronics industry spokesmen discuss the effects
     of Japanese trade and wheat industry
     representatives introduce an argument that the
     policies which protect import-sensitive industries
     adversely affect U.S. wheat exports. Foreign
     trade barriers and their importance as limiting
     access to foreign markets are discussed. General
     comparisons of Japanese and U.S. productivity and
     competitiveness are introduced.

242. United States. Congress. Joint Economic Committee.
     Subcommittee on Economic Goals and
     Intergovernmental Policy. Japanese Voluntary Auto
     Export Limits: Hearing before the Subcommittee on
     Economic Goals and Intergovernmental Policy of the
     Joint Economic Committee, Congress of the United
     States, Ninety-Eighth Congress, First Session,
     October 25, 1983. Washington, D.C.: U.S.
     Government Printing Office, 1983.

These hearings were designed to explore the
voluntary limits which the Japanese Government has
followed for auto exports to the U.S. With the
present relative strength of the dollar as against
the yen, these export limits are an important
means of venting pressure in the U.S. for
imposition of permanent controls. Since foreign
currency fluctuations have such an untoward effect
on particular industries, it is appropriate that
industries like autmobiles should receive some
protection. The auto industry is affected by many
financial factors beyond its control, including
that of the high U.S. dollar. It is argued that
the U.S. is much more liberal in opening its
markets to the Japanese than the Europeans are.
Representatives of the U.S. auto industry testify
that the health of the U.S. auto industry should
not be put into question, but rather that the
breathing spell afforded by import limitations is
a necessary step.

243. United States. Congress. Joint Economic Committee.
Subcommittee on Economic Goals and Intergovernment
Policy. Japan's Economy and Trade with the United
States. Washington, D.C.: U.S. Government
Printing Office, 1985.

This collection of essays examine the Japanese
economy and its relation to the U.S.,
concentrating on their trading relationship. Also
explored are Japanese economic policies of a
domestic nature which affect the U.S. Particular
attention is directed to Japan's industrial
policy, its effects on patterns of trade, on
development, and on structurally depressed and
declining industries. In addition, the U.S. trade
problem with Japan, Japan's foreign exchange
policy, technology transfer, market access in
Japan, and more are discussed.

244. United States. Congress. Joint Economic Committee.
Subcommittee on Monetary and Fiscal Policy.
Japanese and American Economic Policies and U.S.
Productivity: Hearings Before the Subcommittee on
Monetary and Fiscal Policy and the Subcommittee on
Trade, Productivity, and Economic Growth of the
Joint Economic Committee, Ninety-Seventh Congress,
First Session, June 23 and July 28, 1981.
Washington, D.C.: U.S. Government Printing Office,
1981.

The testimony was requested in order to aid the
Congress in developing policies that will
stimulate long-term growth in the U.S. economy.
Japanese and American corporate officials gave
recommendations. The focus was on Japanese

industrial policy, in particular, those measures
which might be applied successfully in the U.S. A
major question was why the Japanese levels of
productivity are higher than those of the American
industries. Speakers presented varied reports and
recommendations.

245. United States. Congress. Joint Economic Committee.
     Subcommittee on Trade, Productivity, and Economic
     Growth. The Legacy of the Japanese Voluntary
     Export Restraints: Hearing Before the Subcommittee
     on Trade, Productivity, and Economic Growth of the
     Joint Economic Committee, Congress of the United
     States, Ninety-Ninth Congress, First Session, June
     24, 1985. Washington, D.C.: U.S. Government
     Printing Office, 1985.

     Japan's voluntary export restraints of 1981 are
     discussed as regards the automobile industry. The
     lack of competitiveness of U.S. businesses is
     noted, and measures to restore its strong position
     are discussed. Statistics on auto prices,
     employment and producer and consumer price indexes
     are offered. Auto industry spokesmen and
     economists' testimony is included.

246. United States. Congress. Senate. Committee on
     Banking, Housing, and Urban Affairs. Subcommittee
     on International Finance and Monetary Policy.
     Foreign Industrial Targeting: Hearing Before the
     Subcommittee on International Finance and Monetary
     Policy of the Committee on Banking, Housing, and
     Urban Affairs, United States Senate, Ninety-Eighth
     Congress, First Session, on Foreign Industrial
     Targeting, Its Results, and Its Lessons for the
     United States, Ceremonial Courthouse,
     Philadelphia, Pa., July 7, 1983. Washington,
     D.C.: U.S. Government Printing Office, 1983.

     The testimony offered was presented at the request
     of the Committee as part of its investigations of
     the effects on the U.S. of foreign industrial
     targeting. Recommendations for the shaping of
     U.S. policy were sought. A central question under
     debate was that of the need of the U.S. to
     initiate similar forms of industrial policy to
     those measures employed by the Japanese. Topics
     include discussion of tax, interest rates,
     productivity, and methods of influencing economic
     growth in Japan.

247. Vandenbrink, John, ed. Corporate Strategy &
     Structure: Japan and the USA. Chicago: Chicago
     Council on Foreign Relations, 1983.

     The U.S. and Japan have been allies who have found

themselves in the position of competing for the
same markets since the early 1970s. Japan´s
relative success has caused the U.S. to begin to
see the Japanese as the designers of an ideally
managed society, mirroring in reverse all that was
wrong with the U.S. at home. There has been a
call for more communication between the U.S. and
Japan to dispel the exaggerated image of Japan in
the eyes of Americans, and to create a better
means of handling trade between the two. Papers
discuss the role of industrial policy in the
context of U.S. institutions, and assess the
Japanese challenge. Other chapters discuss
methods for the U.S. to reduce its problems with
productivity and efficiency. Specific industry
studies are also offered.

248. Vernon, Raymond. <u>Two Hungry Giants: The United
     States and Japan in the Quest for Oil and Ores</u>.
     Cambridge: Harvard University Press, 1983.

     Written in the belief that the national context
     for each country today conditions the range of
     possibilities which their governments may follow
     in economic policy, this book is an analysis of
     the rivalry between the U.S. and Japan. The
     Japanese were a sheltered ward of the Americans
     after the war, and they gradually evolved into
     rivals, with a state of interdependence arising by
     the 1980´s. Facts about the oil market and the
     market in other materials are presented. Then a
     contrast between the U.S. policies and the
     Japanese institutions is offered. Prospects for
     the future depend partly on whether Japan and the
     U.S. both retain their positions of preeminence in
     the world economy. They are likely to do so for a
     few decades yet, and there will probably be
     opportunity for both countries to cooperate or to
     conflict on the issues of raw materials
     distribution.

249. Vogel, Ezra F. <u>Comeback, Case by Case: Building
     the Resurgence of American Business</u>. New York:
     Simon and Schuster, 1985.

     Vogel agrues that Japanese economic power will
     increase and overtake the United States unless a
     strong reply is made. The majority of the book is
     concerned not with a U.S. comeback, but with how
     Japan has been able to adjust to economic crisis,
     restructure its economy, and make investments in
     information and services, putting itself in a
     place to overtake other major world markets by the
     1990´s. A fictitious account is given of the
     demise of U.S. as a competitive power by 1990,
     resulting from an increase in Japan´s share of

nonbasic industries like fiber optics and
biotechnology, as well as service industries like
insurance, retailing, an consulting. The U.S.
government and companies will continue to ignore
the Japanese threat until it is too late. Major
R&D efforts will be kept in Japan and American
plants will be reduced to the status of assembly
operations. Next follows case studies of Japanese
successes in restructuring and industrial policy,
including shipbuilding, coal mining, computers,
and information. U.S. success stories are also
given: the space program, housing, agriculture,
North Carolina's Research Triangle. He ends with
a call for a national strategy, which depends upon
a policy-unified consensus.

250. Vogel, Ezra F. "Guided Free Enterprise in Japan."
     Harvard Business Review. 56.3 (May/June 1978):
     161-169.

     This portrayal of the U.S. and Japanese relative
     economic position examines the mechanisms that
     have enabled Japan to get ahead of the U.S. in
     many industries. Key forces are traced, such as
     the Ministry of Finance, the Ministry of
     International Trade and Industry, the Prime
     Minister's office, the Cabinet, Diet, and
     Keidanren. The role of trade sector
     organizations, union leaders and company
     management is discussed, with attention to the
     financial mechanisms, trade sector development and
     the political process which contributes to the
     business climate. The Japanese system is rated as
     performing better than the U.S. system, but with
     notable undesirable consequences.

251. Vogel, Ezra F. Japan as Number One: Lessons for
     America. Cambridge, Mass.: Harvard University
     Press, 1979.

     This book argues that Japan has become the world's
     leading economic power by means of a conscious
     transformation of the society, in terms of
     government, education, business, the military and
     the law. The many outstanding successes that have
     been made are also balanced by social costs.
     Among those costs are tendencies to conformism, to
     denial of human rights, and to excessive
     nationalism. Other problems, from unemployment to
     crime control are experienced by Japan much as
     they are in the U.S. The assessment of Japanese
     solutions to American problems is given brief
     attention.

252. Weil, F. A. "U.S. Industrial Policy: A Process in
     Need of a Federal Industrial Coordination Board."

Law & Policy in International Business.   14.4
(1983): 981-1039.

This article argued that the basic cause for the
decline in U.S. domestic and international
economic conditions lies in the absence of a
rational industrial policy. U.S. economic
intervention in the past has only been on an ad
hoc basis operating with merely a reactive nature.
Changes in the international economic community,
particularly Japan and Western Europe, necessitate
government involvement in industrial development.
A new Federal Coordination Board is recommended.
This Board would coordinate the complex policies
affecting the industrial sectors, helping to
achieve a stronger international competitive
position.

253. Wijers, G. J.   "Institutional Aspects of
     Industrial Policy."   Journal of Economic Issues.
     16.2 (June 1982): 587-596.

     The current economic crises are causing countries
     to seek new ways of revitalizing their economies.
     Japanese competition is forcing other industrial
     nations to study their industrial structures,
     especially in light of the apparent success of
     Japan´s industrial policies.   Contrary to supply
     side economics, the new institutionalist policies
     seek greater interplay between economic,
     political, technological, and cultural variables.

254. Wolf, Marvin J.   The Japanese Conspiracy: The Plot
     to Dominate Industry Worldwide--and How to Deal
     with It.   New York: Empire Books, 1983.

     In this often polemical work, the author argues
     that Japan is a nation in the grip of an economic
     totalitarianism, dedicated to defeating Western
     competition at any cost and dominating the world
     economy.   This book is more a reflection of the
     swings in American attitudes toward the Japanese
     than an objective contribution to the study of
     Japan.

255. Yamamura, Kozo, ed.   Policy and Trade Issues of
     the Japanese Economy: American and Japanese
     Perspectives.   Seattle: University of Washington
     Press, 1982.

     This volume contains essays on Japanese policies
     and the behavior of firms and individuals, and
     international economic policies.   They are written
     by Japanese and American authors, toward the aim
     of better understanding of the bilateral trade
     situation between the two countries.   The

examination of the role of Japanese firms and
individual begins with an overview, and the
evidence of a decline in the influence of the
government and the increase in competitiveness.
Antimonopoly policy is examined, and changes in
fiscal policy are noted. The role of savings and
investment is described, and the mechanisms for
coping with the oil crisis are traced. Trading
patterns in the steel industry are analyzed, and
the nature of manufactures imports in Japan is
examined. Bilateral exchange rates for the U.S.
and Japan are studied.

256. Zecher, J. Richard, and James Beaver. "If a U.S.
     Industrial Policy Is Needed, Let's Make It Right."
     ABA Banking Journal. 76.4 (April 1984): 130-136.

     This paper argues that proponents of a new U.S.
     industrial policy are incorrect in their desire
     for more government intervention to improve the
     economy. Since the government in not a good
     entrepreneur, it should instead encourage the
     private sector executives to make sound and
     productive choices. This can be achieved by
     implementing monetary and fiscal policies aimed at
     stable prices and economic growth, by creating a
     tax system that encourages savings and
     investments, by a free trade policy, and by
     allowing the markets to determine the allocation
     of resources. Employment, productivity, and
     international trade have been shown statistically
     to have benefitted from private initiatives, while
     Japanese interventionist measures have not had
     lasting results. An industrial policy based on
     private sector leadership will permit economic
     development without disruptions from policy
     changes.

257. Zimmerman, M. A. "U.S. Trade Policy under the
     Reagan Administration." American Chamber of
     Commerce in Japan. 18.4 (April 4, 1981): 18-22.

     This articles focuses on U.S. foreign trade policy
     with Japan, particularly the automobile industry.
     The industrial policies of the two countries are
     compared. The influence of the Reagan
     administration on U.S. economic policy is
     discussed.

258. Zysman, John, and Laura Tyson, eds. American
     Industry in International Competition: Government
     Policies and Corporate Strategies. Cornell
     Studies in Political Economy. Ithaca, N.Y.:
     Cornell University Press, 1983.

     This book consists of seven well-documented case

studies, concerned primarily with particular manufacturing sectors. Three essays deal directly with Japanese competition, covering the fields of color TV´s, automobles, and semiconductors. These cases examine policies that would deal effectively with the decline in U.S. imports and exports. The general opinion by these authors is that the U.S. has adopted a limited policy of protectionism. Recommendations are made for a variety of policies involving growth in productivity, relying on the free market whenever possible.

IV. INTERNATIONAL ECONOMIC RELATIONS

Japan's relations to the international economic community are the focus of this chapter. Japan's influence on the world economy and its impact on the economies and development of individual countries and regions are the subject matters included here. In addition, Japanese domestic policies affecting foreign trade and foreign investments in Japan are presented.

259. Abegglen, James C. The Strategy of Japanese Business. Cambridge, Mass.: Abt Books/Ballinger Publishing Co., 1984.

With the view that the relationship between the U.S. and Japan will remain close even as the trade tensions continue, this book addresses the current state of the U.S. and Japanese economic partnership. An investigation of topics such as the U.S. interest in Japanese management methods, the position of foreign companies in Japan, and technological developments is offered. While the increase in production in Japan has been difficult to accept for many countries, acts of protectionism have been proposed in many areas. The Japanese need for raw materials requires a massive surplus in manufactured goods. Prospects for the future are considered.

260. Akao, Nobutoshi, ed. Japan's Economic Security. St. Martin's Press, 1983.

Discussions in Japan in recent years have begun to develop a broad concept of national security, one which would include the notion of total economic security. This implies a concern for the safeguarding of supplies of key resources, such as energy supplies, which might otherwise threaten economic peace for Japan. An assessment of Japan's resource needs is offered. The oil supply situation is described. The potential for natural gas and nuclear energy is considered, along with the supplies of other minerals and foods. In all, the availability of strategic resources is estimated, and the potential role of Japan in regard to other Asian nations is projected. The role of the pursuit of economic security as it

90

affects the Japanese economic system is also considered.

261. Allen, George C. Japan's Place in Trade Strategy: Larger Role in Pacific Region. London: Atlantic Trade Study, 1968.

Japan's participation in a broad free trade association should be discussed with an awareness of the structure of Japan's foreign trade and the changes that have been occurring in the supply, the markets, and the kind of goods comprising the Japanese imports and exports. This book notes that Japan seems ready to play a larger role in international economic discussions, proposing a Pacific free trade area. Difficulties for the establishment of such associations are large, and would entail the Japanese reliance on greater amounts of food importation. Brief consideration is given to Japanese-British relations.

262. Blumental, Tuvia, and Chung H. Lee. "Development Strategies of Japan and the Republic of Korea: a Comparative Study." The Developing Economies. 23.3 (Sept. 1985): 221-235.

Japan and Korea are considered similar in their recent economic development. Their geographical proximity, the historical ties between them and the success of the Japanese growth pattern must have had a strong effect on the Korean political and economic leadership in formulating Korea's growth strategies. Salient features of the Japanese model of development which apply to Korea are offerred, and the Japanese economy of the 1955-64 era is compared to Korea's economy from 1965-74.

263. Boisot, Max. Intangible Factors in Japanese Corporate Society. Atlantic Papers 50. Paris: Atlantic Institute for International Affairs (Distributed by Rowman & Allanheld), 1983.

The subject of this study is the differences between the corporate strategies of Japan and Western countries. The hypothesis is advanced that cultural factors are important elements in explaining these differences. The Japanese are often perceived as "different", animated by a "Japanese spirit." The question is raised whether Japan is converging with other industrialized nations, or setting its own rules. The notion of convergence is defined and an analytical framework is established. Attention is then focused on the application of this concept to the large Japanese firm, chosen as the most representative

institution since these these firms established
Japan's position in international trade. The aim
of the study is to shed light on how convergence
operates, not so much as an argument for or
against. The forces of divergence appear to have
been predominant in many cultural and business
areas.

264. Brady, Terrence A. "South Korea: `National
Strategy´ and Economic Performance." Review of
Business. 7.3 (Winter 1985): 21-23.

South Korea has become a strong competitor with
the U.S. Korea's economic growth began after the
war in the early 1950's when the U.S. pour large
sums of money into it. Growth was achieved by
reinvesting a sizable portion of its GNP and with
the initiation of a series of 5-year plans in the
1960's under U.S. auspices. These plans called
for the exporting of labor-intensive products. By
the 1970's, Korea was exporting machinery,
transportation equipment, and steel. Korea has
been following the Japanese model of industrial
policy, which targets industries and nutures them
domestically until they can compete
internationally. The Japanese and Korean economic
systems are substantially different from the U.S.,
which place more emphasis on consumers.

265. Brown, C. J. F. "Industrial Policy and Economic
Planning in Japan and France." National Institute
Economic Review (UK). 93 (Aug. 1980): 59-75.

This is an article written by critics of U.K.
planning, in which is proposed the adoption of
certain aspects of Japanese and French planning.
In Japan, the Ministry of International Trade and
Industry (MITI) works very closely with the
private sector. Its industrial policy directs the
economic development, giving priority to
industrial growth. This is achieved by means of
fiscal incentives and the allocation of financial
aid. It works with the central bank to insure
financial requirements are met. MITI also
controls the inflow of imports and foreign
capital. France has had success in setting a
framework for an interventionist industrial
policy. This was originally formulated to deal
with the destruction of World War II, where
decision-makers from various sectors met to
coordinate economic development. Currently,
French planning does not have as strong an
influence as it formerly had. Although the U.K.
has tried these ideas without much success, it is
important to remember the value of coherence aand
strategy in government intervention.

266. Brzezinski, Zbigniew. <u>The Fragile Blossom: Crisis
     and Change in Japan</u>. New York: Harper & Row,
     Publishers, Inc., 1972.

     A report on Japan from a foreign affairs point of
     view, this book offers conclusions on Japan's
     prospects, both domestic and international. A
     general assessment of changes and trends is given.
     Social patterns, including changing aspirations
     and stability of relations are described. The
     political trends are identified. Economic
     prospects, with causes of success and potential
     problems are examined. The international role of
     Japan today and in the future is outlined, in
     terms of relations with various other countries.
     Security and the U.S. relationship are also
     examined.

267. Confederation of British Industry. <u>The Will to
     Win, Britain Must Mean Business: A Discussion
     Document</u>. London: Confederation of British
     Industry, 1981.

     This monograph centers on suggestions for how
     British industry can overcome the present crisis.
     Topics include opportunities and constraints,
     improving international competitiveness,
     alleviating unemployment, economic and financial
     effects, and methods of financing.   Case studies
     are offered on the industrial policy of France,
     West Germany, the U.S., and Japan. Statistics are
     given for 1960-1980.

268. Corbet, Hugh, and Robert Jackson, eds. <u>In Search
     of a New World Economic Order</u>. New York: John
     Wiley & Sons, 1974.

     This is a study of the international trade
     agreements and their liberalization in the period
     of 1972-73. The negotiations of several key
     international bodies are traced, and their
     influence is examined as the key to the trade
     situation for Japan, Europe, and the U.S. Each
     essay in the present volume treats a particular
     field of negotiations, for example, topics covered
     include: diplomacy and crisis, general factors
     affecting negotiations, and issues which exert
     pressure on each nation involved in trade
     partnership negotiations. The energy crisis, the
     strength of multinationals, and world monetary
     reform principles are three such forces. Also
     discussed is the agenda for the three-way
     negotiations which culminated in the Tokyo Round
     negotiations, within the General Agreement on
     Tariffs and Trade. Some issues on the agenda
     included, for example, industrial tariffs,

strategies for modifying non-tariff distortions,
farm-support policies, access for the exports of
developing countries, and adjustment assistance to
import competition. The concluding essay treats
emergency protection against sharp increases in
imports.

269. Czinkota, Michael R., and Jon Woronoff. Japan's
     Market: The Distribution System. New York:
     Praeger Publishing Co., 1986.

     With an insider's view of the distribution system
     in the Japanese economy, this book provides clues
     to foreign businessmen interested in working in
     Japan. The close relationships among Japanese
     businesses are described, as these often make for
     barriers which foreigners cannot penetrate. The
     overall problems in exporting to Japan are traced,
     the specific groupings of Japanese inter-firm
     cooperation are described, and the wholesale and
     retail structure are detailed. Conclusions are
     offered.

270. Diebold, William, Jr. Industrial Policy as an
     International Issue. New York: McGraw-Hill Book
     Co., 1980.

     A product of the 1980's Project of the Council on
     Foreign Relations, this book is written in the
     belief that much more international cooperation
     will be needed in the future to bring about world
     prosperity. In the past, the net effect of most
     industrial policy has been to resist change rather
     than to usher in change smoothly. So the authors
     have undertaken to assess the potential of
     industrial policy from the global point of view.
     Why the goals of growth, stability, full
     employment, choice, and equity, among others, are
     so difficult to achieve rests on the difficulty of
     finding concrete ways to put policies into
     practice. The negative effect of industrial
     policies can be seen in the area of trade
     agreements, their restrictions and
     liberalizations, through tariffs and other
     measures. Industrial policy as applied to
     individual industries is also significant.
     Recommendations for a more positive approach to
     industrial policies are offered and conclusions
     ponder the prospects for the future.

271. Dore, Ronald. Taking Japan Seriously: A Confucian
     Perspective on Leading Economic Issues. London:
     Athlore, 1987.

     Though the British society with its tendency to be
     individualistic and anti-authoritarian is not

similar to Japan´s, this book argues that there
are ways that Japan´s economic success can be a
lesson to Great Britain. Features of Japanese
organization could be imitated, though it is often
group-centered and hierarchical. The
recommendation is offered that the West should
study Japanese methods seriously.

272. Fodella, Gianni, ed. Japan´s Economy in a
Comparative Perspective. Tenterden, Kent,
England: Norbury, 1983.

The Japanese economy is seen in comparison to the
Italian system. Essays relate the performance of
Japan and Italy, since the two nations are of
similar size and forty years ago they maintained
similar economic positions. Yet the changes since
that time have been quite dramatic, with Japan
forging ahead. Important factors involved in
giving the Japanese the edge are identified.
Included are the attitude toward free trade and
protectionism, the flexibility in macroadjustments
of wages and employment, the price markup
equations for manufacturing, and the permanent
employment system. Varied results are offered.
Finance and the size of government deficits are
compared, and regional and external relations are
described.

273. Goldsmith, Raymond W. The Financial Development
of India, Japan, and the United States: A
Trilateral Institutional, Statistical, and
Analytic Comparison. New Haven: Yale University
Press, 1983.

The differing rates of growth of India and Japan
are studied in comparison to the U.S. since 1860,
when the two began their transformations into
modern economies. The U.S. is taken as the
prototype, with India as a slow developing
country, and Japan as a fast developing country.
The aim of the book is to consider the reasons for
these different rates of growth, especially as
they impinge on other nations now beginning to
develop their economic systems. After a chapter
devoted to infrastructure, there are several
treating the financial systems of each country, as
measured through a model using certain simplifying
assumptions. Thus financial interrelations ratios
are computed and compared for Japan and India, and
examined for their explanatory possibilities.

274. Grewlich, K. W. "Industrial Innovation and
Foreign Trade in the 80´s." Intereconomics:
Monthly Review of International Trade and
Development. 16.6 (Nov./Dec. 1981): 269-274.

This article explores the economic and trade
relations between the European Economic Community,
U.S., and Japan. The EEC´s technological
potential is analyzed and the problems it is
having in the fields of cars, steel, textiles, and
agriculture. Technology trade and the barriers to
technology transfer is discussed. Japan´s
industrial policy is review and a call for a
common strategy by the EEC Commission.

275. Grub, Phillip D., et al. East Asia Dimensions of
International Business. Englewood Cliffs, N.J.:
Prentice-Hall International, 1982.

This book emphasizes international business from
an Asian perspective. Changes in financial
structures and export marketing are discussed.
The transnational data flows, and Japanese
productivity are examined. China is studied, and
recommendations for businessmen who wish to better
understand the prospects for Asian business and
for students of Asia are offered.

276. Hedberg, Hakan. Japan´s Revenge. London: Pitman,
1972.

This book offers prognostications for Japan´s
future as the top producing country in the world.
Written from a journalistic point of view, this
book differs from the author´s earlier work, The
Japanese Challenge, by adding strengths as well
as weaknesses to the description of Japan. It
offers a critique of Japanese culture that aims to
be more balanced. There is a need expressed for
Japan to exercise caution, since it is more
important to survive than to win.

277. Helou, Angelina. "Japan and the Tokyo Round."
Journal of World Trade Law (UK). 15.5
(Sept./Oct. 1981): 450-455.

Japan´s participation in the Tokyo Round differed
from its major trade partners in a number of
significant areas. Japan has a large trade
surplus, a close relationship between its
industrial policies and exports, a relatively low
percentage of imported manufactured goods in its
total imports, and unique industrial practices and
organizations which shapes its foreign trade.
There follows a detailed and historical discussion
of Japan´s tariff cuts and their relationship with
quota restrictions since World War II, which
includes a 10 year history of tariff reductions
aimed at reducing Japan´s trade surplus. In
addition non-tariff barriers - restrictions on
foreign currency, import procedures, and

inspection procedures for selected imported products - are discussed in an historical perspective. Lastly, there is a discussion of revising Article XIX of GATT, concerning agreements on industrial safeguards. Japan's particular interest is the specific conditions for selective actions and the role of the surveillance body.

278. Henderson, Dan F. Foreign Enterprise in Japan: Laws and Policies. Chapel Hill: University of North Carolina Press, 1973.

The legal environment for foreign businesses operating in Japan is provided in rich detail. There is an account of the history of foreign enterprise in Japan, and a description of the political dynamics of the economy. The environmental factors in the Japanese social system are delineated, including the nationalist, familial tendencies, and the seniority-based system of compensation. The role of the state and economic planning is also covered. Legal institutions are then described, and the history of legal patterns presented. Details of foreign entry into Japan, with key legal institutions and procedures, are provided, with a discussion of liberalization in international law, counter-liberalization measures and problems with key treaties.

279. Ho, Alfred K. Japan's Trade Liberalization in the 1960s. White Plains, N.Y.: International Arts & Sciences Press, Inc., 1973.

In the postwar period until 1960, Japan followed a conventional policy of economic development with trade controls. After 1960, Japan shifted to a policy of economic development through trade liberalization. This book studies the relationship between trade liberalization and economic development. It compares Japan's economic performance before and after trade liberalization. Two objectives are sought: 1. the effects of trade liberalization on the economic progress of a developing country and 2. lessons that are applicable to other developing countries.

280. Hofheinz, Roy, and Kent E. Calder. The Eastasia Edge. New York: Basic Books, 1982.

Japan, North and South Korea, Taiwan, Hongkong, Singapore, and China are evolving into the world's most productive region. This book outlines the reasons for their new strength. Cultural values, social structures, technology and labor supply are

important factors discussed. The planned use of
capital for development is also considered. There
will be confrontations ahead between the East and
West unless Western nations begin to appreciate
the power of the Eastasia region more fully and
develop better responses to the challenge they are
posing.

281. Hollerman, Leon. Japan's Dependence on the World
     Economy: The Approach Toward Economic
     Liberalization. Princeton: Princeton University
     Press, 1967.

     The purpose of this book is to identify the
     structural difficulties of Japan's economy during
     the process of liberalization in the mid 1960's.
     Some light is cast on the meaning of planning in
     relation to free enterprise in the Japanese
     milieu. The changes in the structure of Japan's
     foreign trade is analyzed in relation to changes
     in the structure of its industrial production.
     Sources of stability and instability in the
     economy are identified. The approach toward
     liberalization is reviewed, with the institutional
     arrangements that brought it about.

282. "Industrial Strategy: For Japan It Works: What
     Lessons for the EEC?" European Trends.   70
     (Feb. 1982): 32-48.

     Problems in trade between the EEC and Japan are
     identified as related to several conditions within
     the Japanese economic system, such as the heavy
     dependence of Japan on manufacturing in the highly
     competitive fields of high tech industries, and
     the relatively low proportion of imports that are
     made up by manufactures. There are also policies
     within Japan that make trade with the EEC
     difficult. The Japanese use cost-cutting and
     strong market presence, for instance. Thus the
     EEC must be careful to avoid protectionistic
     policies and to deal with the actual conditions of
     Japanese trade.

283. Japan. Ministry of International Trade and
     Industry. Industrial Structure Council. Japan in
     World Economy: Japan's Foreign Economic Policy for
     the 1970's, Report of the Industrial Structure
     Council. Tokyo: Ministry of International Trade
     and Industry, 1972.

     This document prepared by the Industrial Structure
     Council of the MITI represents a study of the
     international trade policy of Japan as it relates
     to the overall structure of the Japanese economy.
     The world economy and policies of the 1970's are

treated.

284. Japan Economic Research Center. <u>Japan's Economy
     in 1980 in the Global Context: The Nation's Role
     in a Polycentric World</u>. Tokyo: Japan Economic
     Research Center, 1972.

     The projection of the nature of the Japanese
     economy requires an analysis of the world economic
     environment. Problems for such a projection
     include foreseeing the future of the lingering
     world monetary system, and trends in international
     politics which are not amenable to quantitative
     analysis. But this work attempts to posit the
     changes that can be expected for Japan and the
     world system, as the world becomes polycentric in
     the coming years. The global context is sketched,
     and topics are analyzed in turn: world trade,
     international monetary system, direct investments,
     Japanese resource problems, industrialization of
     the developing nations, and trade system and
     policy.

285. Japan External Trade Organization. <u>White Paper on
     International Trade, Japan 1982</u>. Annual Report.
     Tokyo: JETRO, 1982.

     This report provides an evaluation of Japan's
     foreign trade and its industrial structure in the
     context of Japan's role in the international
     economy. The state of the world economy is
     reviewed with policy prescriptions. Japan's
     industrial policy is examined in light of its
     response to the international economic
     environment. International industrial cooperation
     is discussed as well as exportation and
     importation by commodities. Statistics are given
     for 1970-1981.

286. Japan-Indonesia Colloquium, Ninth. <u>Japan and
     Indonesia in a Changing Environment</u>. Jakarta:
     Centre for Strategic and International Studies,
     1981.

     Papers presented at the colloquium held in
     Surabaya in August, 1981, suggest areas in which
     views from Japan and Indonesia converge or
     diverge. Issues discussed included the problem of
     Japan's industrial restructuring, as this impacts
     on countries in the region, such as Indonesia.
     The security of the region in relation to the
     great powers and the defense policies of Japan
     were also discussed.

287. "Japan's Trade with the EEC: Accommodate or
     Retaliate; Which Way for the Commission?"

European Trends. 67 (May 1981): 19-41.

Japan´s foreign trade with Western Europe is
discussed, reviewing the balance of trade and
invisible trade. In addition Japanese total
import trade by country and by product group is
provided. The impact of Japan´s industrial policy
is analyzed with a comparison of Japanese and EEC
countries´ economies and populations. An EEC
protectionist response to Japanese exports is
discussed. Statistics provided for 1970-1985.

288. Kahn, Herman. The Emerging Japanese Superstate:
     Challenge and Response. Englewood Cliffs, N.J.:
     Prentice-Hall, 1970.

     This book offers wide-ranging assessment and
     predictions about the likelihood of Japan´s
     entrance into the forefront of world politics. In
     judging the recent performance of Japan
     economically, the author sees that Japan now has
     the capability to become a political superpower by
     the end of the 1980´s. The prediction is offered
     that Japan will exercise this option, and that it
     will also become a military power, even acquiring
     nuclear weapons. Much of the book is devoted to
     an assessment of the Japanese mind, including
     summarizations of Japanese political pluralism,
     authoritarianism, communalism and hierarchical
     tendencies. Concepts such as prestige and
     patriotism are also reviewed. The economic
     "miracle" is described, and changes that will have
     to be made if Japan is to step into the limelight
     geopolitically are identified. This situation
     constitutes a challenge to the Japanese people and
     to the Americans, who must be ready to meet the
     Japanese power on its own terms.

289. Kahn, Herman, and Thomas Pepper. The Japanese
     Challenge: The Success and Failure of Economic
     Success. New York: Crowell, 1979.

     The context of the present book is a view of Japan
     as a highly important actor in the economics of
     world affairs, but as a state which nonetheless
     occupies a very modest role politically. How long
     this role can continue to be played successfully
     comes into question. The prospects for Japan in
     the future are systematically explored. Attitudes
     of the Japanese people toward growth are
     investigated. There is also a problem of
     direction that arises for Japan, now that it has
     surpassed the U.S. as the leading nation in per
     capita income. There are institutional problems
     this situation of high success generates, and a
     major debate has insued in Japan as to the

policies for the future. Demographic, housing,
and education trends are outlined, and the growth
of a consumer welfare advocacy is traced. Long-
term prospects for a postindustrial Japan are
offered. Japan's immediate need is developing a
way to take care of excess capacity, and to
conquer the skepticism of the population which
comes into conflict with national goals.

290. Kanamari, Hisao, and Sueo Sekiguchi. The 1974-75
Recession and Economic Stabilization Policy:
Japanese Experience. Japan Economic Research
Center, Center Paper 30. Tokyo: Japan Economic
Research Center, 1977.

This book examines the oil shock of 1973 and its
aftermath, with statistical analysis. Financial
and management policies which led to recovery are
traced. General price rises, domestic demand, and
stagflation are documented, in relation to
exchange rates and international trade. Monetary,
fiscal, labor, foreign exchange and trade policies
are described.

291. Kaplan, Eugene J. Japan's Tariff and Nontariff
Barriers: The Perception Gap. Washington, D.C.:
U.S.-Japan Trade Council, 1979.

There is a difference in the perception of Japan's
openness to trade with the U.S. While the
Americans see Japan as having a closed border, the
Japanese view their markets as open to any country
that wishes to compete effectively. This brief
text reviews the trade agreements between the U.S.
and Japan under the aegis of the General Agreement
on Tarriffs and Trade (GATT.) Non-tarriff
barriers are also described. Factors such as
government procurement, customs, credit terms,
distribution and industrial organization are
mentioned.

292. Kershner, Thomas R. Japanese Foreign Trade.
Lexington, Mass.: Lexington Books, D.C. Heath and
Co., 1975.

This book researches the role foreign trade has
occupied within the Japanese economy. It
concentrates on Japan's complementary relations
with the resource-rich and developing countries of
the Pacific Asian region. Japan's trade network
is a principal explanatory factor behind the
economic success of most countries in this region
from 1965 onward. The two-way trade flows and the
movement of capital from Japan to the Pacific
Asian region are outlined and the economic
relations which have developed since 1960.

293. Kohl, Wilfrid L., ed. <u>After the Second Oil</u>
     <u>Crisis: Energy Policies in Europe, America, and</u>
     <u>Japan</u>. Lexington, Mass.: Lexington Books, D.C.
     Heath and Co., 1982.

     The collection discusses the impact of the 1979
     oil crisis on the Western energy system. Various
     perspectives are offered. Specific energy sectors
     are reviewed, with attention to the role of energy
     in its diferent forms, oil and its alternatives.
     Energy policies of seven industrial countries
     after the second oil crisis are described.
     Japan´s options include conservation, use of
     liquified gas, coal and nuclear power, and
     development of new energy technologies. New forms
     of political participation and protest that have
     emerged are surveyed.

294. Kojima, Kiyoshi. <u>Japan and a New World Economic</u>
     <u>Order</u>. Boulder, Co.: Westview, 1977.

     From the point of view of Japan, a new direction
     for the world economic order is suggested. The
     starting point is the pre-oil crisis situation,
     and then the changes which were initiated in the
     early 70´s are described. Proposals for trade
     agreement rules are made, regarding the Tokyo
     Round negotiations, stressing the positive role of
     tariffs, safeguards, and foreign direct investment
     as the means for each country´s establishment of
     its position. International monetary reform is
     examined. Foreign direct investment is discussed,
     and the different conditions under which Japanese
     and American foreign direct investment is made are
     explained. The long term growth pattern of Japan
     is projected. Finally, proposals for an
     integration of the Asian-Pacific region´s economy
     are presented, developing the suggestions the
     author had presented ten years previously.

295. Kojima, Kiyoshi. <u>Japan and a Pacific Free Trade</u>
     <u>Area</u>. Berkeley: California University Press,
     1971.

     This book brings together revised articles which
     have appeared earlier in a different form. It has
     been assembled with the outlook that the Pacific
     should become a focal point of world economic
     growth, with Japan at the center. The various
     conditions and requirements for this development
     are traced. Japan´s trade liberalization, the
     role of regional free trade efforts, and the
     possiblity for a Pacific free trade area with the
     necessary currency regulations are discussed.

296. Kojima, Kiyoshi. <u>Nontariff Barriers to Japan´s</u>

Trade. Tokyo?: Japan Economic Research Center,
1971.

This discussion of Japan´s trade relationships
concentrates on the difficulties Japan experiences
in entering into import/export exchanges. Often,
it is noted, the barriers are not of a tariff
nature, but of other still effective forms. The
implications of non-tariff barriers to trade and
their future prospects are outlined.

297. Kojima, Kiyoshi, and Terutomo Ozawa. Japan´s
General Trading Companies: Merchants of Economic
Development. Paris: Organisation for Economic Co-
Operation and Development, 1984.

This work concentrations on the activities of
Japanese general trading companies. The top nine
companies are studied in terms of their
investments and activities in developing
countries. Statistics are offered and an
"anatomy" of the structure and functions of the
companies is given. Their roles as
intermediaries, quasi-bankers, information
gatherers and organizers are explored. Topics
include investment, manufacturing, resource
development, and service ventures.

298. Lee, Eddy, ed. Export-led Industrialization and
Development. Geneva: International Labour
Organisation, 1981.

In this book which explores limits on employment
and economic growth in Asian countries, there is a
chapter on Japan´s general trading companies. The
question of the role of general trading companies
as an organizational form is raised, and the
prospects for their use in other Asian countries
is discussed. The nature of general trading
companies is explored, especially as to their
contribution to exports and manufactures from
developing countries. The issue of whether and
how they fit into export-led industrialization in
various Asian countries is discussed.

299. Lipschitz, Leslie, and Susan M. Schadler.
"Manufacturing in Japan and the United Kingdom."
International Monetary Fund Staff Papers. 31.2
(June 1984): 303-38.

By using an econometric model to separate cyclical
and classical influences on manufacturing output
and employment, this article compares the results
for Japan and the U.K. These results, in turn,
are used to compute indices for comparing wage
cost behavior and for drawing analytical

inferences for macroeconomic policy. From this
comparison, an understanding of how different
countries adjusted to the commodity price shocks
of the 1970´s is sought, as well as explaining the
relation of wage adjustments to unemployment
problems and the efficiency of demand management
for increasing output and employment.

300. Manglapus, Raul S. <u>Japan in Southeast Asia:</u>
<u>Collision Course</u>. Washington, D.C.: Carnegie
Endowment for International Peace, 1976.

This book offers an argument as to the impending
conflicts in the Southeast Asia region due to the
Japanese economic growth in the region.
Statistics are presented to document the heavy
Japanese presence. But the style and behavior of
the Japanese business activities is of more
importance in assessing the potential for
conflict. The vertical society models of Japanese
business, the exclusivity of Japanese in relation
to the local workers, and the tendencies for
corruption inherent in the model are used as
primary evidence.

301. Masahide, Shibusawa. <u>Japan and the Asian Pacific</u>
<u>Region: Profile of Change</u>. New York: St Martin´s
Press, 1984.

This book traces the recent developments in the
Asian Pacific, and outlines the course of Japan´s
role there, present and future. Since there is no
homogeneity in the region, Japan´s distinctiveness
is marked. Chronological developments are
treated, and the responses of individual countries
in the region to World War II are noted. An
overview of the economics of the region is
offered, with an assessment of the extent of
Japan´s involvement. The general status of Japan
is examined as it relates to the world in
political, economic, and security terms.

302. Murakami, Yasusuke, and Yutaka Kosai. <u>Japan in</u>
<u>the Global Community: Its Role and Contribution on</u>
<u>the Eve of the 21st Century</u>. Tokyo: University of
Tokyo Press, 1987.

The question of Japan´s contribution to the new
world order is raised. A panel of experts from
Japan deal with the question, concluding that the
Japanese must look toward international
cooperation more seriously. Problems with trade
and other issues threaten to keep them from
exercising their proper world position. Future
considerations are given.

303. Namiki, Nobuyoshi. "Growth of Japanese Exports."
     The Developing Economies. 8.4 (Dec. 1970): 475-
     496.

     The structure of the Japanese balance of payments
     in the decade from 1955-64 was quite different
     from that in the subsequent years, as the balance
     of trade shifted toward big deficits and the
     capital account shifted toward surpluses. Later,
     it has changed into a pattern in which the
     surpluses in the current account due to the
     balance of trade make up for the deficits in the
     capital account. This change was made possible by
     the growth of exports. The rise in growth-
     competitive power has enabled Japan to adopt many
     new economic policies. Various liberalization
     measures and revaluation of the yen are discussed.

304. Niino, K. "On Efficiency and Equity Problems in
     the Industrial Policy - With Special Relation to
     the Japanese Experience." Kobe University
     Economic Review. 19 (1973): 1-9.

     This article provides a comparison of the
     industrial policies of the U.S., U.K., and Japan.
     Focus centers on the Japanese experience,
     emphasizing the unique characteristics of its
     industrial policy especially in terms of its
     handling of efficiency and equity problems.

305. Nomura Research Institute. Investing in Japan.
     London: Woodhead-Faulkner, 1978.

     With the view that the Japanese predicament as a
     resource-poor nation brings certain risks, this
     book deals with changes that Japan now must make
     in order to survive the rise in oil prices. It
     offers an outline of the history and population
     factors leading to the resource imports and import
     dependence in Japan. The labor force, foreign
     trade, balance of payments, fiscal policy and
     industrial policy are described. The structure of
     Japanese companies is given, with analysis of
     certain key sectors. Foreign investments and
     trading companies are described. An introduction
     to the finanacial system is also offered.

306. Okimoto, Daniel I., ed. Japan's Economy: Coping
     with Change in the International Environment.
     Boulder, Co.: Westview, 1982.

     Essays in this collection deal with the position
     of Japan after its attainment of a new status as
     economic superstate. The world order was not
     threatened, even though Japan achieved a
     remarkably fast growth rate, because Japan's new

power was not translated into military power.
World security seemed to be enhanced by Japan's
role. At the same time, problems in the
international economic order did emerge: the oil
crisis, balance-of-payments disequilibria, heavy
recessions, and trade rules changes all had their
effect on Japan. Several perspectives on the
U.S.-Japan relationship are offered, but all of
them include a recognition of the underlying
causes of Japan's trade problems, focusing on the
oil price rise, the fluctuations in the exchange
rate, and the deterioration in Japan's terms of
trade with comparatively high ratio of savings to
dissavings. Some possibilities for the future of
U.S.-Japan relations are offered. Changes in
Japan's financial system are discussed, and also
the reluctance for Japan to become a military
power is examined. In summary, these essays
situate Japan in the current circumstances of the
world economy, which offer significant obstacles
for continued favorable development. Japan's
response will in turn have a profound effect on
the world economy itself.

307. Okita, Saburo. Developing Economies and the
     Japanese Experience. New Delhi: Indian Council
     for Cultural Relations, 1979.

     This book gives the text of a brief lecture noting
     the implications of the Japanese experience for
     India. Non-Western modernization is analyzed
     through the Japanese education system, its
     protection of small-scale industries, and its
     attention to agriculture. Nutritional concerns
     and the need for indiginous technology are noted.

308. Okita, Saburo. Japan in the World Economy.
     Tokyo: Japan Foundation, 1975.

     This work examines the economy of Japan from a
     global perspective. Background observations are
     made, and current trends are identified. The
     political sphere is discussed, with investigation
     of the role that Japan is now playing in the world
     economy. The recent rapid growth and its
     implications are treated.

309. Ozaki, Robert S. The Control of Imports and
     Foreign Capital in Japan. New York: Praeger
     Publishers, 1972.

     This book presents a study of the control of
     imports and foreign capital in Japan since World
     War II. This is one side, the "defensive" side,
     of the Japanese economic strategy. The
     administrative and institutional arrangements that

Japan uses to achieve its control strategy are
described in empirical detail. The legal and
extralegal framework for controls are presented.
Then a review of events that liberalized or
changed the controls is given. Finally a
discussion of Japanese attitudes and positions as
to the merits of pursuing the control strategies
is offered.

310. Ozawa, Terutomo. Multinationalism, Japanese
     Style: The Political Economy of Outward
     Dependency. Princeton, N.J.: Princeton
     University Press, 1979.

     This book illuminates the nature of multinational
     businesses based in Japan, noting that the
     national origin of a firm still has its importance
     even though the firm may be a multinational. The
     multinationals are not actually above the nations,
     nor do they necessarily erode the sovereignty of
     nations. Japan's multinationals are contrasted
     with the U.S.'s multinational experience, to
     uncover the differences between the two. Many
     generalizations that have been made about
     multinationals have been merely extensions of the
     American experience. This book corrects those
     misunderstandings. The emergence and theory of
     the Japanese multinational are described.
     Investment in various areas, resource dependency,
     and conflict with local interests are examined.

311. Reich, Robert B. "The Threat of the Global
     Corporation." Canadian Business. 56.8 (Aug.
     1983): 57-58+.

     The growing number of multinational corporations
     is a major factor in the developing of national
     industrial policies. Two types of multinational
     corporations are discussed. An explanation of
     methods used by Japanese companies to penetrate
     growing markets in developing countries is
     provided, as well as their marketing systems in
     Europe and the U.S. The operations of some
     American multinationals are analyzed with a
     prediction of long-range results. By 1988, 300
     international firms will produce 50% of all goods
     and services, with component parts manufactured in
     various countries. The U.S. must face this
     reality directly, or suffer further economic
     decline.

312. Sadamoto, Kuni, ed. Breaking the Barriers: True
     Accounts of Overseas Companies in Japan. Tokyo:
     Survey Japan, 1982.

     Written to give an overview of the foreign

corporate investments in Japan, this book also
focuses on management, products and personnel
problems. The success of businesses operating in
transnational contexts is recounted. Twenty-two
companies are discussed, having 50% or more
foreign investment. A directory of foreign-
affiliated firms operating in Japan is also
provided. The narratives which cover the
individual firms are direct and detailed.

313. Scalapino, Robert A., ed. The Foreign Policy of
Modern Japan. Berkeley, Calif.: University of
California Press, 1977.

This book presents varied perspectives on the
changing Japanese foreign policy situation. Some
are historical, and others are focused on specific
contemporary aspects of the problem, with the aim
of determining where Japan may be heading. The
essays were the result of a conference held on
Kauai, Hawaii, in January, 1974. Topics
considered include decision-making, public and
private interests, economics and foreign policy,
and security issues. Some conclusions are
offered.

314. Schmiegelow, Michele, ed. Japan's Response to
Crisis and Change in the World Economy. Armonk,
N.Y.: M.E. Sharpe, 1987.

Topics in this collection include foreign
exchange, internationalization of financial
markets, foreign investment, and external aspects
of monetary policy. Also treated are subjects
such as the deficiencies in infrastructure, the
links between the foreign sector and the
macroeconomic performance of the Japanese economy,
the impact of labor policies on export
competitiveness, industrial policy, the relation
between the domestic sales system and imports, and
the changes in official policy toward cartels.

315. Shepherd, G., F. Duch^ene, and C. Saunders, eds.
Europe's Industries: Public and Private
Strategies for Change. Cornell Studies in
Political Economy. Ithaca, N.Y.: Cornell
University Press, 1983.

This report on a research project aims at
identifying the kinds of adjustment problems
facing Western European industry and at
understanding public and private responses to
these challenges. It contains eight sector
studies on textiles, steel, shipbuilding, motor
cars, electrical power plants, process plant
contracting, machine tools, and semiconductors.

The final chapter focuses on Japan's growing
competitive presence and in particular on the
post-war development of the shipbuilding, motor
car and semiconductor industries in Japan.

316. Shinohara, Miyohei. The Japanese Economy and
Southeast Asia: In the New International Context.
Occasional Paper Series 15. Tokyo: Institute of
Developing Economies, 1977.

The Southeast Asia region, and its response to the
Japanese economy is a focus of this work.
Sociological and cultural analysis, as well as the
economic, are considered. Seeing the postwar
growth as Schumpeterian, characterized by high
investment and saving partially induced, the
author describes the changes in the economy during
the 1960's. An analysis of the exchange rate
situation is offered. Future growth prospects are
outlined, with the view that some slowing is
inevitable. In the Southeast Asia-Japan
relationship, more dialogue is advocated.

317. Shinohara, Miyohei, et al. The Japanese and
Korean Experiences in Managing Development. Ed.
Ramgopal Agarwala. World Bank Staff Working
Papers, No. 574; Managememnt and Development
Series No. 1. Washinton, D.C.: The World Bank,
1983.

This comparison of the economies of Japan and
Korea notes that the two countries are similar in
their relatively fast growth, their concentration
on export economies, and their close cooperation
between government and private industry.
Decision-making patterns differ, however, and
Korea relies much more heavily on exports than
Japan. The trade policies of each country are
examined, and the role of competition is treated.
Possible conclusions are suggested with regard to
the transfer of the Korean and Japanese models to
other developing countries, regarding the
importance of prices and competition.

318. Shiratori, Rei, ed. Japan in the 1980s: Papers
from a Symposium on Contemporary Japan Held at
Sheffield University, England September 11-13,
1980. Tokyo: Kodansha International, Ltd., 1982.

The present analysis of Japan is made for the
benefit of the British, with a view toward finding
elements of the Japanese experience that Great
Britain might emulate and learn from. Politics in
Japan are reviewed, with attention to the
electoral system, its foreign policy, defense
debates, and the nature of its democracy.

Economics is treated in an overview, with energy
and fiscal problems, and foreign investment
receiving considerable analysis. Industrial
cooperation is posed as a political subject.
There is also a treatment of political parties in
Japan.

319. Shishido, Toshio, and Ryuzo Sato, eds. Economic
     Policy and Development: New Perspectives. Dover,
     Mass.: Auburn House, 1985.

     This collection of articles begins with an
     argument in favor of the free trade approach to
     the U.S. strategy regarding competing with Japan.
     Then there is a consideration of the more
     developed and less developed countries.
     Fundamental changes in the relative advantages
     enjoyed by the more or the less developed
     determine the positions that each can occupy in
     terms of trade development potential. Another
     chapter treats the tax policies that can be
     pursued with regard to the multinationals. Issues
     in economic development include investment
     criteria, government vs. technocratic management,
     and the positions of China, Thailand, and Hong
     Kong. Productivity in Japan is analyzed, with
     ultra high growth seen as coming to an end.
     Future prospects and the possibility of Japanese
     cooperation with other nations in technologic
     research is appraised. Major essays on industrial
     policy offer conclusions.

320. Shoda, Nagahide. "The `Sogoshosa´ and its
     Functions in Direct Foreign Investment." The
     Developing Economies. 14.4 (December 1976): 402-
     418.

     Characteristics peculiar to the large trading
     companies are delineated. Their foreign trade
     activities are examined. A profile of the
     overseas investments of the trading companies is
     given, in which it is shown that actions differ in
     various regions of the world. Problems they have
     encountered include changing trends in heavy
     industries, decline of their share of foreign
     trade, failures in the consumer goods markets,
     limitation of the indirect financing function, and
     the developing countries´ criticism of
     multinationalization.

321. Shoemack, Harvey R., and Gene DeRoin, eds.
     Japan´s International Trade Policy: Myths and
     Realities. Chicago: Japan Trade Center, 1978.

     Many notions about the Japanese foreign trade
     position have grown up as the Japanese have

rapidly become more successful since the Second
World War. The chief myths surround the Japanese
government's role in the economy and its
international trade policy. This volume
concentrates on dispelling some of the false
images and focusing on current realities.

322. Sinha, Radha. Japan's Options for the 1980s. New
     York: St. Martin's Press, 1982.

     This book is written in the belief that Western
     complaints with Japan are largely unfounded, and
     that a reluctance to restructure Western economies
     to meet changing world realities is at fault.
     Also it seems that the West's anachronistic
     attitudes towards the non-Westerners may be partly
     responsible for the anger that arises when Japan
     appears to be outdoing Western economies. This
     work raises the question of the response Japan
     will ultimately make to this anger. Beginning
     with a review of the impact the war had on Japan,
     the developments of the Japanese economy are
     traced. Foreign trade, the West's criticism, and
     trade liberalization are explored. The
     restructuring of the Japanese economy, and the
     military situation in the Far East with
     concomitant strains on Japanese pacifism are
     discussed. Future options for Japan are then
     entertained.

323. Stokes, Henry. The Japanese Competitor. London:
     Financial Times, 1976.

     Japan is viewed as a competitor to the Western
     nations in the areas of finance, industry, foreign
     trade, and direct investment. Topics discussed
     include the securities market, Japanese
     accounting, dividend policy. Industrial profiles
     of Japan include productivity, profits,
     government-business relations, and activities of
     various specific industries. Foreign trade is
     examined in terms of industrial structure, trading
     companies, and trade with the European Economic
     Community. The discussion of direct investment
     includes relations with Asia, and with regard to
     steel, electronics, and textiles.

324. Takamiya, Susumu, and Keith Thurley. Japan's
     Emerging Multinationals. Tokyo: University of
     Tokyo Press, 1985.

     This book is a commemoration of the life of Makoto
     Takamiya's life and a continuation of his work.
     In addition to economic measurement, the
     understanding of the organizational consequences
     of Japanese overseas investments are sought.

Trying to pin down these consequenses in their
economic, political, legal, sociological and
cultural forms is a major aim of this book. The
essays concern the current state of research on
multinationals, and the "demythologizing" of the
matter.

325. Taylor, Phillip, and Gregory A. Raymond, eds.
Third World Policies of Industrialized Nations.
Contributions in Political Science 76. Westport,
Ct.: Greenwood Press, 1982.

This book introduces the foreign economic policies
that major industrialized nations have used in
regard to the less developed countries. North-
South relations have received considerable
attention as a result of the oil embargo of OPEC
nations. Few books attempt to apply the theories
of foreign policy to the behavior of actual
nations. These chapters treat the actions of
nations at economic summits, including that of
Japan. The concept of preservative adaptation is
used as a theoretical yardstick by which to assess
the behavior of the nations studied.

326. Tsoukalis, Loukas, and Maureen White, eds. Japan
and Western Europe: Conflict and Cooperation. New
York: St. Martin´s Press, 1982.

This book is a collection of essays which examine
the Japanes-European relationship, with some
attention to the American influence as well.
Beginning with the history of European influence
in Japan and mutual images and stereotypes, the
main emphasis is on the economic dimension.
Japan´s economy, industrial policy and politics
are treated. Trade imbalance between the European
Economic Community and Japan, its adjustment,
industrial policies, and foreign direct investment
are then examined as they affect bilateral
relations. Working toward more cooperation, the
final chapter discusses future prospects.

327. Tsurumi, Yoshi. The Japanese Are Coming: A
Multinational Interaction of Firms and Politics.
Cambridge, Mass.: Ballinger Publishing Co., 1976.

The rise of Japanese multinational firms is
changing international economic and political
relations. This in depth study explores Japan´s
emerging relations to the Asian region and the
Third World and how the Japanese multinationals
are going to affect the world wide oligopolistic
powers that the U.S. and European-based
multinational firms have established in
manufacturing industries and in the exploitation

of natural resources. Unlike American and
European-based multinationals, Japanese
multinationals have grown from small and medium-
sized firms, have included trading firms as
partners in manufacturing ventures, and have used
direct investments as vehicles for the
international transfer of manufacturing technology
and managerial skills. The motivations for
Japanese companies to go multinational are
analyzed in the context of Japan's internal
political and economic situation in the postwar
period. The factors responsible for Japan's
success are rapidly changing, requiring revision
of its industrial strategy and institutional
arrangements from education to government-business
relations. Experiments carried out to tackle the
problems raised by Japanese multinational firms
are examined with the objective of predicting
future courses of actions open to these firms.

328. Tsurumi, Yoshi, and Rebecca Tsurumi. Sogoshosha:
     Engines of Export-Based Growth. Montreal:
     Institute for Research on Public Policy
     (Distributed by Renouf/USA), 1980.

     This is a description of the large trading
     companies of Japan which includes a history and a
     profile of their current operations. The internal
     workings, current problems and survival stragegies
     are examined. The potential for them to
     contribute to U.S. and Canadian development and
     trade is assessed, and models for "sogososha" for
     U.S. and Canadian firms are outlined. The ability
     of the large trading companies to use specialized
     market knowledge, an ability to make deals which
     interlock, and the introduction of small and
     medium sized firms to foreign trade are described.

329. Ueno, Akira. "Trade and Capital Liberalization
     Policy of Japan in the Sixties and Adjustment of
     the Japanese Industry." Management Japan. 18.1
     (Spring 1985): 8-11.

     Making Japan's industries competitive
     internationally has been accomplished in the case
     of shipbuilding, steel, and electronics through
     the efforts of industrial policies. In
     electronics, key firms were promoted by the
     government through low-interest loans and
     encouragement of investment. Since the government
     had targeted this industry for growth, its lending
     policies had considerable success in making an
     almost tenfold growth rate take place in just over
     twenty years.

330. United States. Congress. House. Committee on Ways

and Means. Subcommittee on Trade. Task Force
Report on United States-Japan Trade, with
Additional Views. Washington D.C.: GPO, 1979.

This report finds that bilateral trade would be
normalized between Japan and the U.S. with the
elimination of certain trade barriers. Japan is
moving toward opening markets other than high
technology and agriculture. The introduction of
more Japanese investment in the U.S., creating
more jobs, is regarded as desirable. American
structural problems are identified as causes of
the trade imbalance, and Japanese trade barriers
are considered of secondary importance.

331. United States. Congress. House. Committee on Ways
and Means. Subcommittee on Trade. United States-
Japan Trade Report Prepared for the Subcommittee
by its Chairman and the Members of its United
States-Japan Trade Task Force. Washington D.C.:
GPO, 1980.

Trade imbalance between the U.S. and Japan is
studied. The means of opening the Japanese market
to more U.S. exports are discussed, including the
Strauss-Ushiba agreement of 1978. Barriers to
U.S. entry into the markets are also considered,
and topics discussed include cartels, banks,
transportation equipment and Japanese government
policy. Various means of promoting U.S. exports
are considered. The option of restricting
Japanese imports into the U.S. is seen as
undesirable.

332. United States. General Accounting Office. United
States-Japan Trade: Issues and Problems; Report by
the Comptroller General of the United States.
Washington D.C.: U.S. General Accounting Office,
1979.

This report discusses the success and failure of
U.S. firms which have attempted to penetrate
Japanese markets. The study was prompted by the
U.S. trade deficit problem arising in 1976-78.
Broad factors underlying the deficit are
identified. Case studies from seven industries
are offered. Reduction in Japanese protectionism
with regard to industries other than
telecommunications is noted, yet slow adjustment
to this change seems to have taken place in U.S.
industry. Factors that affect the performance of
U.S. and Japanese firms are discussed. The
contrasting trade policies of the two countries
are examined.

333. Uri, Pierre, ed. Trade and Investment Policies

for the Seventies: New Challenges for the Atlantic
Area and Japan. New York: Praeger Publishers,
1971.

While there appears to have been progress made in
the establishment of world trade, disappointment
is evident as to the lack of success in removing
the final barriers that remain after the Kennedy
Round. High tariffs, quota restrictions, and
nontariff barriers remain. The relations between
Japan and other countries have not been fully
normalized, and the developing countries´ pressure
for industrialization has not been handled
satisfactorily. Other obstacles also plague the
nations engaged in setting up such agreements.
This book explores the future of international
trade, its worldwide options, and the role of
Japan. Japan´s role regarding the other
industrialized countries, its general trading
companies, and its trade and investment policies
are examined.

334. Vernon, R. "Japan´s Industrial Policy in an
Interdependent World." Oriental Economist.
42.764 (June 1974): 14-17.

This article provides an overview of the
internationalization of the world´s industries and
its effects on Japan´s industrial policy. Joint
ventures are playing an important role in this
process. A look is taken at the case of oil in
industrial policy. Changes in the Japanese
economy are examined, along with Japanese
cooperation with foreign interests.

335. Warnecke, S. J., ed. International Trade and
Industrial Policies: Government Intervention and
Open World Economy. London: Macmillan, 1978.

While this collections of essays mainly discussed
government support and subsidies for the U.S.,
Canada, and the EEC countries, it does include one
on Japanese subsidy policies. In addition there
are other articles discussing subsidies and other
industrial aids, the international effects of
subsidies, and the negotiation of rules on
subsidies.

336. Wilks, Stephen, and Maurice Wright. Comparative
Government-Industry Relations: Western Europe,
United States, and Japan. Cambridge: Oxford
University Press, 1987.

The conflict between the rule of the marketplace
and the logic of government is discussed. Recent
research on government-industry relations is

presented. A comparative overview of the West
German, French, British, U.S. and Japanese systems
is given.

337. Woronoff, Jon. Asia's "Miracle" Economies.
     Armonk, N.Y.: M.E. Sharpe, Inc., 1986.

This book gives a general treatment of the fast
developing economies of Asia. Japan's role as an
investor in the region is considered, and its
relations with host countries is investigated.
The context of neocolonialism is portrayed with a
new world order in view.

338. Woronoff, Jon. Japan's Commercial Empire.
     Armonk, N.Y.: M. E. Sharpe, Inc., 1984.

An attempt is made to objectively present the
working of Japan's international economic
relations, clearing up exaggerated images of the
Japanese as greedy exploitors or as kind and
generous capitalists. Japan's rapid economic
growth and international commercial relations are
reviewed, looking at their foreign operations and
their relations with host countries, particularly
the third world. The book explores the
requirements for Japan's economic growth: growing
markets, continuous supplies of raw materials, and
the employment of foreign labor to work their
world factories. Japanese international
investments are discussed in the context of
neocolonialism, of their relationship to Japan,
and of a new international commercial order quite
distinct from Japan's earlier, prewar empire.

339. Woronoff, Jon. World Trade War. New York:
     Praeger, 1984.

This book is written in the belief that free trade
is a principle that should be followed more
strictly by today's nations. The many cases in
recent times when trade conflicts have arisen are
discussed in detail, industry by industry.
Attention is given to the exporters, and
importers, as well as to the different
perspectives of developed and developing nations.
Frequently the author notes that the facts demand
that blame for recent trade imbalances and
disruptions must be given to Japan, and to other
countries secondarily, because they have not been
strong enough economically to resist Japan's
imposition of its will. Without the use of
sophisticated economic analysis, this book points
out that trade conflicts are the product of
differences in economic policy and the
contradictory material interests that result.

340. Yoshihara, Kunio. <u>Japanese Economic Development:</u> <u>A Short Introduction</u>. Cambridge: Oxford University Press, 1979.

Japan is of interest to competitors and nations interested in receiving more Japanese aid. This book, written for college course use, gives a history of Japan's economic development. It puts Japan's capitalism in a comparative economics framework, and accounts for the changes in the trade patterns that are noted over time. An analysis of Japan's development then leads to an evaluation of the desirability of using Japan as a model for other countries to follow. Problems such as the poor working conditions in factories, the unequal distribution of income, and the high levels of industrial pollution are cited as part of the "pathology" of growth. Imperialism and militarism are also cited. The relative merits of socialist and capitalist systems for countries like Japan are discussed.

341. Yoshihara, Kunio. <u>Sogo Shosha: The Vanguard of</u> <u>the Japanese Economy</u>. New York: Oxford University Press, 1982.

The importance of sogo shosha, trading companies, in the development of Japan's foreign trade and economic success is the theme of this study. The meaning of sogo shosha is defined in their international context. The history of the most important companies (Mitsubishi Shoji, Mitsui Bussan, and others) is given from their foundations in the late 19th century to the present. An analysis of their evolution in the functioning of the economy is outlined along with their dismantlement by American officials after the war and their reformation by MITI in the 1950's. An examination is presented of the reasons for the business success of these trading companies, of their contributions to the industrialization of Japan, of the nature of their management, and of their function in modern Japanese society. Besides providing trading services, they have aided in arranging technology transfers, have provided banking functions, and have considerable political influence.

342. Yoshino, Michael Y. <u>Japan's Multinational</u> <u>Enterprises</u>. Cambridge, Mass.: Harvard University Press, 1976.

This book presents the Japanese version of the multinationalizing trend in business evolution. Elements particular to the Japanese process are isolated and analyzed in their historical setting.

The evolution of Japan's oil industry is reviewed
with its overseas ventures and government
involvement. The spread of manufacturing into
developing and advanced countries is discussed as
well as investments in the U.S., Japanese trading
companies, and Japan's strategies toward foreign
direct investment. The manufacturing firm is
analyzed in terms of its international divisions,
its changing strategies, and ownership policies,
and is seen to be converging with its American
counterpart. In the area of management, the
Japanese and American methods and practices are
distinctly different.

343. Yoshino, Michael Y., and Thomas B. Lifson. The
     Invisible Link: Japan's Sogo Shosha and the
     Organization of Trade. Cambridge, Mass.: M.I.T.
     Press, 1986.

     This book studies the sogo shosha (trading
     companies) as a Japanese business institution.
     Topics discussed include the historical evolution
     of sogo shosha, their distinctive capabilities and
     economic function, and the types and dynamics of
     competitions they face. The internal working of
     these trading companies is also explored. A
     number of organizational managerial aspects and
     practices are covered: organizational structures,
     administrative processes, human resource systems,
     career patterns, the use of interpersonal networks
     as a primary channel and tool of management,
     interunit coordination, and interfirm
     coordination. A look is taken at the challenges
     facing the sogo shosha in the modern Japanese
     economy and society.

344. Young, Alexander K. The Sogo Shosha: Japan's
     Multinational Trading Companies. Boulder, Co.:
     Westview Press, 1979.

     Japan's multinational trading companies are
     analyzed. Their business methods, sales and
     profit trends, strategies, national influence, and
     future prospects are described. The structural
     characteristics of these multinationals are
     outlined, in contrast to the prewar structures and
     to Western multinationals. The role of these
     multinationals in Japan is explained as importers
     of food, raw materials, and equipment, and as
     exporters of Japan's goods. They are important as
     a force behind Japan's economic system, because
     they are influencing the distribution of goods
     domestically and the investments in international
     natural resource development programs.

V. TECHNOLOGY AND INDUSTRIAL POLICY

Technological innovation has played an essential role in Japan's economic success. Japanese industrial policies are often geared toward the promotion of technological developments in specifically targetted industries, especially high-tech fields. Individual industries and their policies are presented here.

345. Anderson, Alun M. <u>Science and Technology in Japan</u>. Longman Guide to World Science and Technology. Essex: Longman Group Ltd, 1984.

This textbook discusses science in modern Japan. Beginning with two chapters of overview, the role of government in promoting science is explored carefully, in the context of the various agencies which are actively involved. Education and the universities are described. Industrial research and development is discussed, as well as agriculture, medicine, and energy. Transportation, electronics, and various environmental sciences are outlined, including a study of earthquake and disaster prevention. International and professional science organizations are described, with an appendix listing the major research establishments.

346. Baranson, Jack. <u>Robots in Manufacturing: Key to International Competitiveness</u>. Mt. Airy, Md.: Lomond, 1983.

This assessment of the design, production, marketing and employment of robots in Japan, the U.S., and Europe is the result of this business executive's study. It includes the guidelines for competing in the robotics industry, and analyzes factors that determine the rate of automation taking place in various countries. Selected companies are profiled.

347. Borrus, Michael, James Millstein, and John Zysman. <u>U.S.-Japanese Competition in the Semiconductor Industry: A Study in International Trade and Technological Development</u>. Policy Papers in International Affairs 17. Berkeley, Calif.: Institute of International Studies, University of

ɔrnia, 1982.
nt title: <u>International Competition in</u>
<u>ced Industrial Sectors: Trade and Development</u>
<u>e Semiconductor Industry, a Study prepared</u>
<u>he Use of the Joint Economic Committee,</u>
<u>ress of the United States</u>.

The United States' loss of its lead in the
semiconductor industry has serious repercussions,
since semiconductors are at the heart of computer
technology, and the U.S. held dominance in the
field for twenty-five years. This book depicts
the evolution and operation of the U.S. and
Japanese semiconductor industries, showing that
national differences make major contributions to
the international competitiveness of each country.
The question of the Japanese entrance into the
U.S. market, with the utilization of its
controlled domestic market is discussed, as
typical of the economic struggle between advanced
countries. Some consideration is given to the
reconciliation of the U.S.'s drive to restore its
lead in the field with the interests of the
European nations.

348. Calton, Jerry M. "Industrial Policy,
International Competitiveness, and the World Auto
Industry." <u>Journal of Contemporary Business</u>.
11.1 (June 1982): 63-82.

This paper reviews the industrial policy for the
world automobile industry. In Europe, policy has
involved tariff and nontariff barriers, the
creation of the European Economic Community, and
nationalization. Japan's auto industry policies
include protection of the domestic market,
technology transfer, and government assistance.
The world automobile market is becoming integrated
by the commonality of consumer preferences, by
decreasing trade barriers, and by shrinking
regional differences in cost and productivity.
Recommendations for aiding innovation in the U.S.
auto industry are: 1) patent laws revision, 2)
government acquistion of patent rights industry
usage, 3) joint public and private sector
research, 4) dissemination of public financed
research to private industry, and 5) encouragement
of private investment in high-risk technology.

349. Carter, Charles, ed. <u>Industrial Policy and</u>
<u>Innovation</u>. National Institute of Economic and
Social Research, Policy Studies Institute and
Royal Institute of International Affairs. Joint
Studies in Public Policy 3. London: Heinemann
Educational Books Ltd, 1981.

With one chapter on the Japanese experience, this book features a study of the role of British government in promoting innovation for industry. A survey of industrial policies, and an outline of technology and research and development are offered. The role of the National Enterprise Board and the extent to which industrial policy can affect change are described. Institutions, markets and policies for micro-electronics in Europe are studied.

350. Chang, C. S. The Japanese Auto Industry and the U.S. Market. New York: Praeger Publishing Co., 1981.

In the attempt to analyze some of the forces that have contibuted to making the automobile market in the U.S. available to the Japanese manufacturers. A history of Japanese auto manufacturing in a non-technical vein is offered. The data are obtained from a review of the literature primarily before 1973. The second part of the book develops the background for the U.S. auto market. Recommendations for the industry are given.

351. Cole, Robert E., ed. The Japanese Automobile Industry: Model and Challenge for the Future? Michigan Papers in Japanese Studies 3. Ann Arbor: Center for Japanese Studies, The University of Michigan, 1981.

These essays assess the role of Japanese market penetration in the U.S. auto industry, as a factor in the recent decline of U.S. competitive strength. It is found to be just one of many complex forces which combine to produce the current situation. Issues such as the American industry's future, the perspective of government, business and labor, the status of U.S.-Japan trade agreements, and the role of labor are addressed. The U.S. legislative response to auto industry unemployment is discussed, as well as industrial policy and quality control measures in Japan. The roles of technology and management are also examined.

352. Cole, Robert E., and Taizo Yakushiji, eds. The American & Japanese Auto Industries in Transition: The Report of the Joint U.S.-Japan Automotive Study. Tokyo: Technova, Inc., 1984.

With a background of trade imbalance and friction between Japan and the U.S. since 1979, this book identifies the conditions that will allow the two countries to work together for the prosperity of both nations' automobile industries. Factors

include the consumers´ demands, flexible
manufacturing systems, rapidly evolving
technology, and the internationalization of the
automotive industry. Adjustments to the
competitive forces at work must be sought within
several key areas: macroeconomic policy, exchange
rate, market access, technological progress,
manufacturing cost differences, manufacturer-
supplier relations, human resource management, and
public policy.

353. "Computer Industry Slowly Narrowing Gap with
     Counterparts Abroad." Trade and Industry of
     Japan. 23.4 (April 1974): 26-32.

     This is a summary of a white paper on computers
     for 1973 by the Japan Computer Usage Development
     Institute. It reviews the structure of the
     computer industry and government policy toward the
     industry. A global system of computers is
     explored with its ramifications on social systems.

354. De la Torre, Jose. Clothing-Industry Adjustment
     in Developed Countries. New York: St. Martin´s
     Press, 1984, 1986.

     This book examines the protected clothing
     industries of developed countries, in order to
     understand the background of the complex system of
     protection against the exports of textiles and
     clothing from LDC´s to OECD countries. An
     assessment is made of the question of whether the
     clothing industries of OECD countries would
     disappear without rigorous protection. Analysis
     of private and public responses to change in the
     clothing industries of the U.S., Japan and the EEC
     shows that successful companies in the these
     countries have already demonstrated a route to
     survival by serving an increasingly international
     and fashion-oriented segment of the market.
     Government policies need to support the efforts of
     those companies that are moving in line with
     global market trends.

355. Doe, P. "Why the U.S. Is Playing `I´ve Got a
     Secret´." Electronic Business. 10.4 (April 1,
     1984): 66,68.

     The Japanese press see the development in the U.S.
     of a protectionistic industrial policy. Aimed at
     Japan, it would protect U.S. technology from
     Japanese competition. The flow of information
     between Japan and the U.S. has become more
     restrictive, for example by National Security
     regulations. The Japanese have also been excluded
     from scientific/technology meetings. In general

the U.S. is becoming aware of the need to protect
its leading industries from Japanese competition
by stopping the free flow of information.

356. Eto, Hajime, and Konomu Matsui, eds. R & D
Management Systems in Japanese Industry.
Amsterdam: North-Holland, 1984.

The interest in Japanese innovation leads to a
need to study R&D management systems and
strategies in Japan. Many implicit comparisons
between Japanese and Western nations are offered.
Consisting of reports of activities in various
industry, some analysis and review is also
presented. Computer development strategy is
traced, and innovation guidance systems are
explained. Public investment in R&D is examined
and creativity is discussed. Information
technology innovation and trends in patents are
outlined. The conflict-resolution methods in
Japanese R&D work are examined.

357. Fairlamb, David. "Public Policy Issues and the
Technological Revolution." Banker (UK).
131.662 (April 1981): 113-115.

Governments in Western Europe, Japan, and North
America are becoming more concerned with promoting
technological change in a manner that does not
conflict with public policy priorities. Even
conservative institutions are becoming aware of
the possibilities of microtechnology. This
technology has already had a wide impact on the
financial sector. This sector rerpesents a huge
potential market for computerized systems.
Governments are recognizing the importance of
microtechnology and telematics for their
industrial policies. Because of their potential
even market-oriented organizations are interested
in stimulating the microelectronics industry and
protecting it from foreign competition.

358. Feigenbaum, Edward A., and Pamela McCorduck. The
Fifth Generation: Artificial Intelligence and
Japan's Computer Challenge to the World.
Reading, Mass.: Addison-Wesley Publishing Co.,
1983.

Although the American computer industry has been
innovative and successful, the Japanese consider
the computer industry vital to their economic
future and have set national goals to be number
one by the 1990's. Japan's Ministry of
International Trade and Industry has formulated
far-reaching strategies and plans in what it calls
Fifth Generation Computer Systems. Implementation

of the plan began in April 1982 with the
establishment of the Institute for New Generation
Computer Technology and coordinated laboratories
of major Japanese companies in the computer
industry. Even if the Japanese do not succeed in
all the objectives of their ten year plan,
partially realized concepts superbly engineered
can have enormous economic value, capture the
market, and place Japan in a dominant position.
This book studies the anatomy and technology of
the computer and knowledge industry in light of
Japan's competitive strategy. In response the U.S.
needs a national plan to adequately confront the
Japanese challenge.

359. Gerstenfeld, Arthur, ed. Technological
     Innovation: Government/Industry Cooperation. New
     York: Wiley-Interscience Publication, John Wiley &
     Sons, 1979.

     Beginning with the importance of technology for
     economic growth in Europe, this book discusses
     general issues raised by the cooperation of
     government in the introduction of technology.
     Mostly concentrating on the European experience,
     the theoretical and empirical consequences of
     technology on industry are explored. A chapter on
     Japan is devoted to a discussion of the effect of
     government policy on innovation. The social
     background, research and development, human
     resources, international trade in technology,
     information systems, and future prospects are
     delineated.

360. Gregory, Gene. The Japanese Propensity for
     Innovation: Electronics. Institute of
     Comparative Culture Business Series Bulletin 86.
     Tokyo: Sophia University, 1982.

     It came as a surprise to many when Japanese
     computer firms were able to surpass other nations
     in very large scale integration (VSLI) technology.
     This development, which took place at the end of
     March 1980, was the product of more than 100
     researchers. And while the research and
     development cost that went into the project was
     relatively modest, not a large percentage of GNP,
     communications technology also took major strides.
     Public and private expenditure data, the tendency
     to innovate, and the role of tax policies and
     competition in Japan are presented. The overall
     conclusions indicate that the Japanese tendency to
     encourage innovation through its educational
     system and within its industrial management
     structure is a key reason why Japan has made such
     progress. Its highly competitive business

environment, and its successful management of
human resources are also important factors.

361. Gregory, Gene. "Japan's Telecom Industry Rushes
     into the Information Age." Telephony. 206.20
     (May 14, 1984): 138-150.

     The privatization of Nippon Telegraph & Telephone
     Public Corp., the launching of Japan's first
     operational communications satellite, and the
     arrival of optical fiber production will have
     profound social effects. For over a decade, the
     Japanese have been committed to the development of
     communication and information technologies. They
     have developed optical fiber communications for
     railways, subway systems, and expressways.
     Improvements in microwave communications,
     satellite service, and digital switching systems
     have enhanced transmission capabilities and the
     speed of communications. Japanese equipment
     manufacturers are increasing their production for
     foreign markets. NEC, Fujitsu, and Oki are now
     producing automatic branch exchanges (PABX) in the
     U.S.

362. Ike, B. "The Japanese Textile Industry:
     Structural Adjustment and Government Policy."
     Asian Survey. 20.5 (May 1980): 532-51.

     The Japanese government policy toward the textile
     industry is reviewed from the perspective of the
     theory of adjustment assistance. This theory
     seeks means of reducing the private and social
     costs of adjustment, thereby reducing the need for
     other methods of protection. Japanese economic
     policy decision-making and the government's
     assistance record to the textile industry is
     discussed. Policy alternatives and additional
     possibilities of finding multilateral solutions
     are explored.

363. Imai, K. "Iron and Steel: Industrial
     Organization." Japanese Economic Studies. 3.2
     (Winter 1974/75): 3-67.

     This article analyzes the structure and function
     of Japan's iron and steel industry, as well as the
     distortions arising from the government's
     industrial policy. An overview of the industry's
     growth is given for the period 1955-1972. Various
     aspects of the market structure are covered:
     oligopoly, differentiation, economies of scale,
     concentration, and entry barriers. The tendency
     toward cartelization and the cartel in investment
     is discussed in light of the investment and
     pricing adjustment processes. The Yawata-Fuji

merger is examined as a case study. Future
prospects are reviewed.

364. Ishihara, Hideo. "Energy Demand and Supply
     Conditions in Japan." OPEC Review, Vienna. 8.3
     (Autumn 1984): 283-308.

     Japan's postwar economic growth was predicated on
     the availability of abundant and cheap imported
     oil. In almost every industrial sector a shift
     was made from coal to oil. In the U.S. and
     Europe, there was a reluctance to undergo rapid
     change in order to protect domestic coal and crude
     oil production. The oil industry's development
     and changes in the industry's environment are
     analyzed. Trends in electric utilities are
     reviewed. The outlook for Japan's long-term
     energy demand and supply is provided. Statistics
     are given for 1970-1987.

365. "Japan's Strategy for the 80s." Business Week.
     2718 (Dec. 14, 1981): 39-120.

     An overview is provided of Japan's industrial
     strategy for the 1980's. The internationalization
     of the Japanese economy requires structural change
     and financing of a new technology strategy. The
     Japanese seek world market leadership in consumer
     electronics and are developing a strategy for the
     computer market. They are making advances in
     electronics research, focusing on fifth generation
     computers. U.S.-Japanese competition is
     discussed, along with the possibility of opening
     the Japanese market to foreign suppliers in the
     communication markets. A look is also taken at
     robot exports and developments in the
     biotechnology industry.

366. Kawahito, Kiyoshi. The Japanese Steel Industry:
     With an Analysis of the U.S. Steel Import
     Problem. Praeger Special Studies in
     International Economics and Development. New
     York: Praeger Publishers, 1972.

     Written with the view that more quantitative
     analysis of the Japanese steel industry is
     required for a full understanding, this book
     begins with a survey of the postwar development of
     the industry. Production, markets, materials,
     distribution, pricing and other factors are
     presented. A computer model is then presented to
     explain the earlier pattern of the steel trade
     between the U.S. and Japan, and to project trends.
     The study should help the U.S. steel industry and
     others to better assess the role it is likely to
     play in current world markets.

367. Keegan, Warren J. "International Competition: The Japanese Challenge." Journal of International Business Studies. 15.3 (Winter 1984): 189-193.

Japan's competitive victories over U.S. and European firms in basic and high-tech industries has produced research into Japanese business practices concentrating on government/business cooperation, R&D, savings rates, quality circles, productivity, and financial strategies. This study however focuses on their approach to strategic market planning and its effects on the competitiveness of their firms. There is essentially nothing new or secret here. Generally, the Japanese avoid simplistic solutions to complex problems. It is recommended that Western companies return to the basics of the application of known principles and procedures, action, and hard work. Industrial policy and government-business cooperation is discussed.

368. Knight, Arthur. "Government Intervention: Its Impact on the Textile Industry." Journal of General Management (UK). 3.1 (Autumn 1975): 11-19.

This is essentially an article on the negative effect of the British government's policies toward textile industry technology from 1955 to 1960. In particular policies toward importation, competition, and employment are analyzed. Thus the government lack clear definitions of economic criteria in dealing with developed and less-developed countries. French and Japanese industrial policies unite economic, trade, employment, and regional development into a coherent policy. The U.K. should take heed and set their policies by a consensus approach.

369. Kreinin, Mordechai E. "United States Trade and Possible Restrictions in High-Technology Products." Journal of Policy Modeling. 7.1 (Spring 1985): 69-105.

The U.S. world market share in high-tech products is declining relatively to Japan and the EEC. This can be explained mainly by the increase of the human capital/labor endowment ratios of Japan and Germany and not by their industrial policies. It is a mistake to lump together the high-tech industries under a single set of policy initiatives, because there are major differences and requirements among these industries. The U.S. should make massive investments in human capital and in research and development and not increase trade restrictions. An effort similar to the one

taken after the U.S.S.R. launched Sputnik should
be undertaken.

370. Long, Theodore Dixon, and Christopher Wright, eds.
     Science Policies of Industrial Nations: Case
     Studies of the United States, Soviet Union, United
     Kingdom, France, Japan, and Sweden. New York:
     Praeger Publishers, 1975.

     Adding to the already large amount of material on
     the role of science in the U.S. economy, this book
     introduces other powerful countries and outlines
     the various positions that are taken regarding
     centralized control of science versus a balance
     between freedom and control. The chapter on Japan
     illustrates how the linkages between science,
     technology, history and ideology give a unique
     slant and direction to the Japanese experience. A
     strong evolutionary dimension is offered by the
     acknowledgement of the continual change that
     accompanies high levels of industrialization.
     Science policy is conceived as practice of the
     scientific method by a diverse community
     including pure inquiry and application for profit
     or welfare.

371. Manning, R. "The Race For Technological
     Leadership Hits the Straight." Far Eastern
     Economic Review. 127.4 (Jan. 31, 1985): 56-59.

     The future economic and scientific leadership of
     the world may depend on winning the competitve
     struggle over supercomputers and 5th generation
     artificial intelligence. The Japanese are
     producing new machines to challenge American
     supercomputers. Although the Japanese caught up
     quickly with American technology, experts believe
     the U.S. can continue to lead. The Reagan
     administration has even developed an industrial
     policy in this area, allocating over $200 million
     to research and $650 million to the Pentagon for
     artificial intelligence projects. An analysis of
     their market and uses is provided.

372. McAbee, M. K. "Japan is Rethinking its Industrial
     Structure." Chemistry and Engineering News.
     53.4 (Jan. 27, 1975): 13-21.

     The current oil price increase is causing Japan to
     rethink its industrial policy. Within the next
     ten years, Japan plans to reduce its dependence on
     energy-intensive industries. This will result in
     an industrial structure significantly different
     from today´s Japan with much more emphasis on high
     technology industries. It further entails
     promoting overseas investments. Suggestions are

made regarding Japanese resource allocation.

373. McLean, Mick, ed. <u>The Japanese Electronics
Challenge</u>. Technova Seminar on Microelectronics,
1980 and 1981. New York: St. Martin's Press,
1982.

Improved technology in microelectronics is
expected to yield solutions for some of the
present world economic difficulties, such as low
economic growth, unemployment and inflation. As a
component of economic change, technological
innovation will have significant effects on
society and everyday life. The essays here
concern the future role of microelectronics for
Japan and Europe. Social and political
implications, and the influence of
microelectronics on other technologies are
considered. The effects of microelectronics on
social welfare and the economy as a whole are also
treated. Discussions are presented.

374. McLean, Mick, ed. <u>Mechatronics: Developments in
Japan and Europe</u>. Westport, Ct.: Technova,
Quorum Books, 1983.

The combination of microelectronics and mechanical
engineering, mechtronics is a new technology with
a major impact. These papers explore the
scientific and economic possiblities of the new
technology as well as the wider social
implications. Japan's lead in the field, the role
of mathematics, and the new management of
production are examined. Office and domestic
applications are presented, and also advanced
consumer products. Semiconductor technology and
robots are studied. The development of
information technology and total firm productivity
is explored.

375. Moritani, Masanori. <u>Japanese Technology: Getting
the Best for the Least</u>. Tokyo: Simul Press,
1982.

Industrial technology has been a major area of
Japanese government-business cooperation in its
domestic development and importation. Japan no
longer simply imports and adapts foreign
technology, but has become a leader in high-tech
fields such as fibre optics, VTR's, and semiconductors. Japan's strength arises from its
ability to miniaturize, to integrate different
processes and products, and to link the
development, design, and production of high-tech
products at low prices with a relatively high
level of quality. A description of the business

environment is given which fosters the development
of Japanese technology. The nature of corporate
management and labor relations are considered to
be major factors in contributing to Japan's
success, as well as the involvement of the
Ministry of International Trade and Industry in
the promotion of technological innovation. There
is also a discussion of lack of funding in basic
research, a weakness Japan is working to overcome.

376. Mowery, David C., and Nathan Rosenberg.
     "Commercial Aircraft: Cooperation and Competition
     Between the U.S. and Japan." California
     Management Review. 27.4 (Summer 1985): 70-92.

     The Japanese commercial aircraft industry has not
     had the same kind of "catch-up" industrial policy
     that the Japanese government has applied
     successfully to other industries. The threat to
     U.S. dominance of the commercial aircraft
     international market is exaggerated. The limited
     size of Japan's domestic aircraft market has made
     it dependent on collaborating efforts with U.S.
     and European firms in developing engines and large
     transport planes. It is unlikely that Japan will
     emerge as an independent competitive force in the
     near future. However, multinational consortia are
     becoming more prevalent in the development and
     production of aircraft, indicating that the
     framework for joint ventures needs to be
     reexamined.

377. Mowery, David C., and Nathan Rosenberg. The
     Japanese Commercial Aircraft Industry Since 1945:
     Government Policy, Technical Development &
     Industrial Structure. Occasional Paper of the
     Northeast Asia-United States Forum on
     International Policy, Stanford University.
     Stanford: Stanford University Press, 1985.

     This short monograph discusses the Japanese
     government's industrial policy towards the
     commerical aircraft industry in the postwar
     period. It describes the aircraft industry's
     structure, its technological development, and how
     the government aided its growth.

378. Niksch, Larry A. A Study of the Relationships
     between the Government and the Petroleum Industry
     in Selected Foreign Countries: Japan.
     Washington, D.C.: U.S. Government Printing Office,
     1975.

     Variant Title: National Fuels and Energy Policy
     Study.

This is a short report prepared by the
Congressional Research Service on the Japanese
policies toward its petroleum industry. It was
prepared at the request of Henry M. Jackson,
Chairman, Committee on Interior and Insular
Affairs, United States Senate, pursuant to S. Res.
45, the national fuels and energy policy study.

379. Okimoto, Daniel I. Pioneer and Pursuer: The Role
of the State in the Evolution of the Japanese and
American Semiconductor Industries. Occasional
Paper of the Northeast Asian-United States Forum
on International Policy, Stanford University.
Stanford, Calif.: Stanford University, 1983.

This book gives a comparison of the U.S. and
Japanese approach to developing the semiconductor
industry. The expense of technology and the
financing of research and development is
considered. The role of innovative behavior is
treated. The different roles of the state in the
two countries are depicted.

380. Okimoto, Daniel I., et al., eds. Competitive
Edge: The Semiconductor Industry in the U.S. and
Japan. ISIS Studies in International Policy.
Stanford, Calif.: Stanford University Press, 1984.

A comparative study of the American and Japanese
semiconductor industry by a binational working
group. The aim is to present an objective
analysis of the intensifying competition between
the two countries in order to prevent a serious
and harmful confrontation. It moves beyond the
allegations and perceptions of both sides to
understanding the actual dynamics of the
competitive struggle in semiconductors. It
concentrates on the basic technology, financial,
and poltical factors affecting the competitive
relationship between the two countries.

381. Oshima, Keichi. "Technological Innovation and
Industrial Research in Japan." Research Policy:
A Journal Devoted to Research Policy, Research
Management and Planning. 13.5 (Oct. 1984): 285+.

A description is given of the industrialization
process in the Meiji era, the technological
development of Japanese industry after World War
II, and the industrial research which supported
development and innovations in the 1980's. Two
major factors in promoting the growth and
development of the Japanese economy have been the
government's industrial policy for promoting
innovation and the private sector's innovative
enterprises. Overviews of various trends are

given: industrial production and the export of
industrial products; technological development
capacities, compared with other OECD-countries;
R&D contributions by the private sector and the
government; trade in technology by sectors; and
the composition of Japan's microcomputer club
members. Statistics are offered from 1950-80.

382. "Outline of New Textile Industry Policy: Making
the Industry More Knowledge Intensive." Digest
of Japanese Industry and Technology. 196 (1984):
7-9.

This article offers a summary of various aspects
of a new textile industry policy, the promotion of
which is planned by the Japanese government. The
purpose of the policy is to deal with changing
environments which the industry is encountering
both at home and abroad. The promotion of
development and the introduction of new
technologies are aspects of the new policy.
Expansion of structural improvement means and the
promotion of internationalization and increased
demand for silk goods are also features of the
policy.

383. Patrick, Hugh, and Larry Meissner, eds. Japan's
High Technology Industries: Lessons and
Limitations of Industrial Policy. Seattle, Wa.:
University of Washington Press, 1986.

This collection of essays focuses on Japanese high
technology industry and its industrial policy.
Articles included are "Japanese high technology
industrial policy in comparative context" by Hugh
Patrick; "Regime characteristics of Japanese
industrial policy" by Daniel I. Okimoto;
"Industrial policy and factor markets:
biotechnology in Japan and the United States" by
Gary Saxonhouse; "Japan's industrial policy for
high technology industries" by Ken-ichi Imai;
"Joint research and antitrust: Japanese vs.
American strategies" by Kozo Yamamura; "Technology
in transition" by Yasusuke Murakami; and "Japanese
high technology policy: what lessons for the
United States?" by George Eads and Richard Nelson.

384. Phillips, Richard, and Arthur Way. Auto
Industries of Europe, U.S. & Japan to 1990.
Economist Intelligence Unit Special Series 3.
Cambridge, Mass.: Abt Books, 1982.

In a detailed study of the U.S. automobile
industry which finds many problems and perils
ahead, the heart of the findings indicate that the
U.S. lags behind Japan in its management. This

implies that the Japanese are superior in knowing
how to combine people, machinery, and raw
materials for production of a quality, low-cost
product. Increased competitive position for the
U.S. implies therefore a thorough and full-scale
improvement of all facets of the management now in
place. This is not possible on the basis of any
single maneuver, but requires a penetrating and
full reorganization. The present condition of the
workforce management is described, along with
details of the recent past. Three cases are
considered as possibilities for the future. In
one, new designs for small cars bring back the
U.S. auto industry. In another scenario, the U.S.
industry is dismantled and taken abroad. And in
the final one, complete restructuring brings back
innovative technology and the U.S. takes the lead
again.

385. Pinder, John, ed. National Industrial Strategies
and the World Economy. Atlantic Institute for
International Affairs Research Volume. London:
Allanheld, Osmun & Co., 1982.

The essays are written with the view that the
adaptation of industrial structures to meet the
needs of the international market is difficult and
complex. The world system for production and
trade in manufactures is traced, and types of
industrial policy are reviewed. Recent events in
five key industrial sectors are given. Policy
responses of governments and international
organizations are assessed. Industrial policies
of Japan, the U.S., Canada and Western Europe are
examined.

386. Rosenbloom, R.S., and W. J. Abernathy. "The
Climate for Innovation in Industry." Research
Policy: A Journal Devoted to Research Policy,
Research Management and Planning. 11.4 (Aug.
1982): 209-225.

Policy factors are examined that may have
influenced innovative vitality of U.S. consumer
electronics industry during the post World War II
period. Successful innovations are analyzed to
reveal what factors might explain the relatively
sluggish performance of American firms in contrast
to Japanese ones. The role of management
attitudes and practices is studied. Statistics
are offered for 1948-1978.

387. Rothwell, Roy. "Public Innovation Policy: To Have
or to Have Not?" R & D Management. 16.1 (Jan.
1986): 25-36.

In the last decade, many governments became
concerned with increasing the rates of industrial
technological innovations through specific policy
formulations. The question is asked whether these
policies were necessary. In the case of the U.S.,
these policies are not essential in achieving high
rates of industrial innovation and a new high-tech
industrial sector. Informal policies have proved
practical. On the other hand, Japan's
international competitiveness has benefitted from
its formal and comprehensive innovation and
industrial policies. Innovation policies appear
to derive from political and cultural processes
unique to one country and cannot simply be
transferred to another.

388. Runyan, L., et al. "The Power Behind the
     Policies." Datamation. 26.12 (Dec. 1980): 176-
     191.

     A review is given of the policies used to promote
     the computer industry and data processing support
     schemes in West Germany, United Kingdom, France,
     and the United States. The U.S. computer trade,
     production, and market shares are discussed in the
     context of Japanese projects, funding, market
     shares and import duties.

389. Sadamoto, Kuni, ed. Robots in the Japanese
     Economy: Facts about Robots and Their
     Significance. Tokyo: Survey Japan, 1981.

     There is a general treatment of robots in Japanese
     industry, from their social and political
     implications, to their technical role. The
     structure of the sectors using robots is examined,
     and the demand for them is outlined. The economic
     and competitive power of robots is described. A
     consideration of the classes of technological
     development is offered, with a discussion of the
     use of robots by smaller firms. The future for
     research and development of robots in Japan is
     assessed.

390. Sanderson, Fred H. Japan's Food Prospects and
     Policies. Washington D.C.: Brookings
     Institution, 1978.

     This paper is written with the view that the
     reliance on imported foods by Japan has caused
     some concern for policymakers. It is argued that
     the recognition of Japan's continuing need for
     agricultural interdependence in the future should
     be planned. U.S. food stocks should be offered to
     Japan with the assurance that adequate supplies
     will continue. At the same time, agreements by

the Japanese to cooperate with the U.S. in
determining improved access to its markets should
be extended. World food supplies are described,
and policy in Japan, with options, are examined.
The management of interdependence is discussed.

391. Semiconductor Industry Association. The Effect
     of Government Targeting on World Semiconductor
     Competition. Cupertino, Calif.: Semiconductor
     Industry Association, 1983.

     A case history is provided describing Japanese
     industrial strategy for the semiconductor
     industry. An analysis is offered of the effects
     of industrial targeting on international
     competition in semiconductors, and in particular,
     the cost to the U.S. industry.

392. Souda, Katsuhiro. "The Changing Alcoholic
     Beverages Industry in Japan." Business Japan.
     30.8 (Aug. 1985): 41-45.

     Trade restrictions and conditions pertaining to
     liquor sales are described. Shipment volume has
     increased approximately 23% in the last 10 years.
     Annual per-capital consumption of alcoholic
     beverages in Japan is increasing. Beverages
     containing an alcoholic content of 1% or more are
     subject to tax, and liquor tax revenue amounted to
     nearly 5% of the national tax revenue in 1983.
     Japan's distribution routes for alcoholic
     beverages are relatively simple, and the volume of
     Japanese imports is almost twice that of exports.

393. "Studies Identify Challenges to U.S. High Tech
     Leadership." Business America. 6.9 (May 2,
     1983): 7-11.

     The role of high technology industries in the U.S.
     for economic and military security is reviewed.
     Their importance for output growth, productivity
     and trade performance is discussed, analyzing the
     factors contributing to the decline in U.S.
     leadership. Recommendations are made to prevent
     further decline of the U.S.'s international
     competitiveness. Industry targeting is mentioned
     with a look at the industrial policies of the
     U.S., Japan, France and West-Germany.

394. Sun, Chen, and Chi-Yuan Liang. "Energy Policies
     of the ROC, ROK and Japan: A Comparison."
     Industry of Free China. 54.3 (Sept. 1980): 2-
     16.

     The effects of the oil crisis on the economies of
     Taiwan, South Korea, and Japan are discussed. An

outline is given for the supply and demand of
primary energy from 1954-89. Planning for future
energy supplies is described, including the
pricing policy for oil and industrial policy that
is relevant to energy economics.

395. Tatsuno, Sheridan. The Technopolis Strategy:
Japan, High Technology, and the Control of the
Twenty-First Century. New York: Prentice Hall,
1986.

This book treats the high technology developments
of recent years and offers projections as to the
strategy Japan will be following. High technology
industries are reviewed, and technological
innovation is discussed. The research and
development institutes in Japan, and the
government's policy regarding science and industry
are also treated.

396. Tran, Van Tho. "Industrial Policy and the Textile
Industry: The Japanese Experience." Journal of
Contemporary Business. 11.1 (1982): 113-128.

The textile industry in Japan is an example of the
successful integration and cooperation between
export/import policies and industrial policy.
Through consistent management of the textile
industry, through its various historical stages in
Japan, the Japanese have developed a balanced
relationship with the other countries in Asia.
Their policies have stressed free trade, careful
monitoring of the textile industry domestically,
aid to failing firms, and use of an international
labor pool.

397. Tsunemi, T., and K. Fukuda. "Trends of Textile
Machinery Industry." Digest of Japanese Industry
and Technology. 172 (1982): 3-16.

Two presentations are offered of the current
trends in the technical field within the Japanese
economy since 1973. Production and export
patterns are given, with discussion of exports by
region, domestic demand, production orders, and
industrial policy. The spinning, weaving and
knitting machinery industries, along with the
dyeing and finishing machinery industries are
described, with statistics from 1974 to 1981.

398. Uneo, Hiroya, and Hiromichi Muto. "The Automobile
Industry of Japan." Japanese Economic Studies.
3.1 (Fall 1974): 3-90.

In this assessment of Japanese industrial policy,
the automobile industry is featured with its

attractions and problems. The MITI's protection
policy is examined in relation to the auto
industry. Competition's role and the nature of
industrial reorganization are outlined.
Differences in earnings and profits are traced.
The efficiency and public responsibility of
industry are outlined, in relation to enterprise
groups.

399. United States. Congress. House. Committee on Ways
and Means. Subcommittee on Trade. Japanese
Voluntary Restraints on Auto Exports to the United
States: Hearings before the Subcommittee on Trade
of the Committee on Ways and Means, House of
Representatives, Ninety-Ninth Congress, first
session, February 28 and March 4, 1985.
Washington, D.C.: G.P.O., 1985.

Representatives of automobile dealers,
manufacturers, and importers appeared to address
the Committee regarding Japanese voluntary
restraints in automobile trade. Statements by
other citizens and congressmen were also taken.
Voluntary Japanese restraints on the export of
automobiles to the U.S. were due to expire in
March, 1985. These restraints had been in place
since 1981, in response to a desire to give U.S.
auto manufacturers a "breathing space," in which
to make the transition to new competitive
conditions. Arguments are offered as to whether
to call for the extension of the restraints or to
allow them to expire.

400. United States. International Trade Commission.
Competitive Factors Influencing World Trade in
Integrated Circuits: Report to the Subcommittee on
International Trade of the Committee on Finance
and the Subcommittee on International Finance of
the Committee on Banking, Housing and Urban
Affairs of the United States Senate on
Investigation. Washington, D.C.: U.S. Government
Printing Office, 1979.

This report analyzes factors affecting the present
and future international competitive position of
U.S. producers of integrated circuits. Production
and foreign trade data on integrated circuits is
provided for the years 1974-1978. Analysis is
offered of foreign government involvement in the
IC industry, comparing foreign and U.S. government
policies. Japan and Western Europe are included
with a discussion of trade barriers.

401. Wilson, Robert W., Peter K. Ashton, and Thomas P.
Egan. Innovation, Competition, and Government
Policy in the Semiconductor Industry. A Charles

River Associates Research Study. Lexington,
Mass.: Lexington Books, D.C.Heath and Co., 1980.

Major changes in the semiconductor industry have
brought about far more expensive technology,
demanding new methods of financing. In many
countries the government has become involved, and
the U.S. must evaluate its policies toward the
industry. Its changing role is examined, and the
effects of policies on semiconductor firms
depending on their resource base, product mix,
innovative behavior and competitive strategies is
acknowledged. Relevant questions include the role
of policy for demand and supply, corporate goals,
organization, strategy formation, and performance.
Each of these is examined systematically.

402. Wu, Yuan-li. Japan's Search for Oil: A Case
     Study on Economic Nationalism and International
     Security. Hoover Institution Publication 165.
     Stanford, Calif.: Hoover Institution Press, 1977.

     With the aim of preserving the postwar alliance of
     Japan and the U.S., this book points out
     difficulties that should be avoided in the course
     of Japanese-American relations. Its focus is the
     1973-74 oil crisis, and the nature of the Japanese
     response. Japan's policy shift, though perhaps
     with hindsight it can be considered an over-
     reaction, gave a tangible example of how Japan's
     policy changes in crisis. The policy consisted of
     diversification, autonomous supply development,
     expansion of foreign exhange receipts, and
     monetary restraint and reduction of oil
     consumption. Adverse effects on Japan's relations
     with other nations can be expected from these
     policy actions. Long-run possiblities are
     explored.

403. Yamauchi, Ichizo. "Long-Range Strategic Planning
     in Japanese R and D." Futures. 15.5 (Oct.
     1983): 328-341.

     The differences in the industrial policy and
     strategy that are evidenced among the Western
     nations can be explained in terms of the
     historical stages of industrialization. An
     examination of Japanese industrial policy shows
     that the Japanese relied on government direction
     of its economic development, with a liberal use of
     technologies already being practiced elsewhere.
     Thus Japanese research and development profitted
     from advances that were developed in other
     countries, and the Japanese could import
     technology without incurring the risks of
     developing it for themselves. Before the 1970's,

Japanese industries did not need to create new
technologies, thanks to this historical situation.
But it is now important for Japan to become a
leader in research and development, since it has
met its goals for industrial growth since the
1970´s.

VI. FINANCE AND FINANCIAL ORGANIZATION

This chapter includes material describing the workings of Japan's financial system, its role in economic growth, and its function as a source of investment incentives. The money and capital markets, monetary policy, and fiscal policies are discussed in relation to industrial policy and government economic intervention.

404. Adams, Thomas F. M., with the collaboration of Iwao Hoshii. A Financial History of Modern Japan. Tokyo: Research, Ltd., 1964.

A rewrite of the author's 1953 _History of the Japanese Securities Markets_, this book gives a financial history and the background of the demand for and acquisition of capital. The development is comparable to Western economies' history, but remarkable for its rapid growth. The formation and consolidation of capitalism, maturity of capitalism and wartime situations are followed by details of the postwar financial situation.

405. Adams, Thomas F. M., and Iwao Hoshii. A Financial History of the New Japan. Tokyo: Kodansha International, 1972.

This long book covers the financial underpinnings of Japan's rapidly growing economy. An analysis gives an account of the financing of trade and industry, the credit system, and many financial institutions. The Occupation is recounted, with the changes in financial situation, from wartime inflation to recovery. The institutional developments are discussed, including the banking system, securities companies, and stock exchanges. The period of rapid growth is presented in terms of structure, fiscal policy, the capital market, the call money market and consumer credit. Finally the era of internationalization is covered, including the position of Japan, its role in finance, and foreign business in Japan.

406. Bronte, Stephen. Japanese Finance: Markets and Institutions. London: Euromoney Publications, 1982.

Japan´s monetary system was modernized during the
1970´s, with the introduction of entirely new
instruments and markets. Investment and trade
controls were liberalized, with significant
international effects. These changes can be
expected to continue. The book details the
changes which are underway. Types of financial
institutions are identified, and their aims and
means of operation are described. Japan´s
financial markets are then examined in detail,
with their evolution and organization.
Predictions are offered for the future movement of
current trends. Statistical data are primarily
from the year 1980.

407. Emery, Robert F. <u>The Japanese Money Market</u>.
     Lexington, Mass.: Lexington Books, D.C. Heath and
     Co., 1984.

     This book is a study of the Japanese money market,
     its main participants, and the types of
     instruments used. The postwar period is the
     focus. Background material is offered on the
     institutional framework and how the money market
     relates to these institutions. There is a survey
     of the whole system, and an explanation of the
     money market brokers´ role. Historical trends
     since 1945 are outlined. The rate of growth of
     the market and its major components are given.
     The various money market instruments are analyzed
     in detail, and trends for the future are
     identified.

408. Emi, Koichi. <u>Government Fiscal Activity and</u>
     <u>Economic Growth in Japan, 1868-1960</u>. Institute of
     Economic Research. Hitotsubashi University.
     Economic Research Series Tokyo: Kinokuniya
     Bookstore Co., 1963.

     With an awareness of the idea that the role of
     Japan´s government has often been stressed as the
     dominant reason for its economic success, this
     writer has compiled data from the original records
     of public finance. The statistical comparisons
     which must underlie the theoretical analysis of
     the role of government fiscal activity in the
     growth of the economy are offered. Both revenue
     and expenditure by the government are relevent to
     this study, but in this volume only the government
     spending aspect is covered. Emphasis is placed on
     the prewar period, with historical observations
     that are of value for analysis of the postwar
     period.

409. Federation of British Industries. <u>The Japanese</u>
     <u>Economy</u>. London: Federation of British

142   Postwar Industrial Policy in Japan

Industries, 1962.

This pamphlet is designed as an introduction to
the structure of the Japanese financial and
economic system. The potential for Japan as a
trading partner with Britain is explored, and the
trade policies of Japan are investigated. Japan's
market is systematically discussed, in terms of
its general operating conditions, the inflow of
foreign capital and technology, the consumer goods
sector, and the various licensing agreements and
investments of British firms in Japan. Data on
the growth of the Japanese economy are offered as
background.

410. Feldman, Robert A. Japanese Financial Markets:
Deficits, Dilemmas, and Deregulation. M.I.T.
Press, 1986.

This book analyzes the major innovations in
Japan's financial markets over the last fifteen
years. It examines how Japan's fiscal deficits
and current swings have created self-perpetuating
cycles of innovation and deregulation in financial
markets. Using portfolio theory the author
presents material on debated issues, including the
extent of the internationalization of Japan's
capital market and how monetary policy reacts to
innovations.

411. Goldsmith, Raymond W. The Financial Development
of Japan, 1868-1977. New Haven: Yale University
Press, 1983.

This book studies the financial development of
Japan from 1868 to 1977. The author divides these
years into six periods (chapters): 1. Out of
Middle Ages: 1868-1885, 2. The takeoff into
sustained economic growth: 1886-1913, 3. The
uncertain trumpet: 1914-1931, 4. Riding for a
fall: 1932-1945, 5. Paradise regained: 1946-1953,
and 6. The Japanese miracle? 1945-1975. Extensive
use is made of statistical data. Basic changes in
the infrastructure set the framework for the
analysis of financial institutions; money, prices,
and interest rates; and capital formation, saving,
and sectoral financial surpluses and deficits.
Overviews are provided for financial assets and
liabilites and the national balance sheet.

412. Hama, Atsushi. The Yen-Dollar Relationship,
Macro-Economic Policy, Financial and Capital
Markets and Related Issues. Tokyo: Keidanren,
1983.

This book responds to various criticisms, mainly

from Americans, regarding the "undervalued yen," and its treatment by the Japanese. It offers an objective basis from which to make discussions, since both sides of the argument require some detailed understanding of the financial markets. The meaning of the yen's devaluation for Japan, with its trading position is discussed. Causes are identified. Measures taken by Japan are outlined, and actions of the U.S. in response are examined. Conclusions are posed.

413. Horne, James. Japan's Financial Markets: Conflict and Consensus in Policymaking. Sydney: George Allen & Unwin in association with the Australia-Japan Research Centre, Australian National University, 1985.

Based on detailed analysis of Japan's financial markets, this book centers on the interrelations of the political system in Japan with the agencies of the government. The Liberal Democratic Party and the Ministry of Finance are studied in particular, to determine how they interact in developing regulatory policy. The reasons why regulations are designed must be gleaned from such study. Topics treated include the establishment of the CDs market, the trade in government bonds, the postal savings system, foreign exchange law, and the developments in the yen-bond market from 1970-82. An institutional overview, and a survey of it, is also offered.

414. Ikemoto, Yukio, et al. "On the Fiscal Incentives to Investment: The Case of Postwar Japan." The Developing Economies. 22.4 (Dec. 1984): 372-395.

This paper questions the thesis that fiscal incentives were granted uniformly to all industries and thereby failed to gear the allocation of resources toward any specific group of industries. The utilization of incentives may have been uneven across industries, and there is no clear proof that fiscal incentive policies affect corporate behavior in such a way as to achieve the intended results. These claims are examined with statistical evidence on the postwar Japanese fiscal incentive policies, to test the effectiveness of fiscal incentive policies in promoting investment.

415. "Japanese Industrial Policy." OECD Observer. 69 (April 1974): 20-26.

This article provides a description of the way in which the Japanese industrial policy is formulated and implemented. Methods of financing industrial

development are discussed with an outline of the
major objectives of Japan's industrial policy. A
general review is given of the growth in Japanese
manufacturing production.

416. Kawaguchi, Hiroshi. "The `Dual Structure' of
Finance in Post-War Japan." The Developing
Economies. 5.2 (June 1967): 301-328.

The high growth rate of the Japanese economy after
World War II was accelerated by financial
concentration, and thus it has been necessary to
impose strong credit rationing continuously on the
medium and smaller enterprises. From this emerged
a dual structure of finance. It is the aim of
this paper to divide this dual structure into two
aspects, the dual structure of borrowers and the
dual structure of lenders, to explain how these
structures came into existence, and, at the same
time, to attempt some theoretical analysis
regarding the meaning of "credit rationing" in
these contexts.

417. Kawaguchi, Hiroshi. "`Over-loan' and the
Investment Behavior of Firms." The Developing
Economies. 8.4 (Dec. 1970): 386-406.

The keen competition in investment between private
firms in Japan produced a very high ratio of fixed
capital formation to GNP during the 1950s and
1960s. Japan was able to quickly overtake all of
the other nations. Investment behavior which
accounts for this remarkable progress is analyzed.

418. Lin, Ching-Yuan. Japanese and U.S. Inflation: A
Comparative Analysis. Lexington, Mass.: Lexington
Books, D.C. Heath and Co., 1984.

Causes for the diverse experiences of the U.S. and
Japan in terms of price increases are sought.
Inflation subsided in Japan after the first oil
shock, while it increased in the U.S. The U.S.
recession was of shorter duration, yet Japanese
price stabilization was achieved at the cost of
losses in output and income as compared to the
potential. The evolution of both economies before
and after 1974 is traced. The role of each
country's economic policy is examined. If
acceleration in inflation is caused by excess
demand, there is no doubt that tightening of
monetary policy is appropriate. But controversies
in timing the policies remain. When inflation is
the result of increased import prices, this policy
is questionable. Other policies are recommended
for this scenario.

419. Monroe, Wilbur F. Japan: Financial Markets and
     the World Economy. New York: Praeger Publishers,
     Inc., 1973.

     This book investigates important topics in the
     area of the Japanese financial system. The
     effects of the 1971 international monetary crisis
     and the exchange market crisis are explored. The
     role of the Tokyo Foreign Exchange Market is
     examined. The various financial instruments and
     their internationalization are studied, including
     the short-term money markets, bonds, stocks, and
     government securities. Foreign banks and direct
     investments in Japan are outlined. Various
     implications of Japanese financial power for the
     world economy and for the future stability of
     international relations are assessed.

420. Patrick, Hugh. Finance, Capital Markets, and
     Economic Growth in Japan. New Haven, Conn.:
     Economic Growth Center, Yale University, 197?.

     This paper discusses the role the Japanese finance
     system, and its capital markets, played in Japan's
     rapid economic growth in the postwar period.

421. Patrick, Hugh T., and Ryuichiro Tachi, eds. Japan
     and the United States Today. New York: Center on
     Japanese Economy and Business, Columbia
     University, 1987.

     The implications of new developments in the
     international financial and economic environment
     are explored. Since 1985, volatile changes have
     occurred. Key features are exchange rates,
     macroeconomic policy, and financial markets.
     These topics are explored in the context of U.S.-
     Japan relations. Tensions between the two
     countries are assessed for their importance to
     international economic relations.

422. Pressnell, L. S., ed. Money and Banking in Japan.
     Trans. S. Nishimura. London: Macmillan, The
     Credit Information Co. of Japan, 1973; Tokyo: The
     Bank of Japan, 1969.

     The general monetary structure of Japan dates back
     100 years or so, and has been maintained to some
     degree through the great changes of the recent
     period. The degree of development of the capital
     market is related to the role of the banks in
     Japanese finance. The break-up of monopolies
     since the war and the introduction of more
     competition and decentralization is noted. The
     postwar "Dodge Line" changed the financial
     arrangements which had brought inflation and heavy

government financing of industry and favored
instead the role of banks. The structure of the
banking industry in Japan is described. Levels of
investment and saving are examined and the
importance of the banking system is assessed.
Public finance and existing financial institutions
are described at length.

423. Rybczynski, Tad M. "Industrial Finance System in
Europe, U.S. and Japan." Journal of Economic
Behavior & Organization. 5.3-4 (Sept./Dec. 1984):
275-286.

For several years, industrial finance has been
debated in academic, financial, industrial, and
political fields. Discussions have focused on
various aspects of the subject, including the
function of financing arrangements in macro- and
micro-policies, particularly in regard to
industrial policy. In the broad context of the
evolution of financial systems, the methods of
providing external finance to firms in the U.S.,
Europe, and Japan is described. Reasons for
differences in financial systems are discussed
along with the attitudes of policymakers to the
evolution of financial systems. From a
Schumpeterian perspective, an attempt is made to
theoretically unite the evolution of financial
systems and financing arrangements to firms, the
process of economic change, capital accumulation,
and risk-taking.

424. Shibata, Tokue, ed. Public Finance in Japan.
Tokyo: University of Tokyo Press, 1986.

This book was written by Japanese officials and
scholars to provide a comprehensive and balanced
outline of Japanese public finance. As Japan's
exports continue to expand, problems in trade
friction increase. The economy is criticized from
abroad. This book presents information to ease
that criticism. The role of the public sector,
the development of public finance, and the
national finance administration are described.
Other topics include the general account budget,
the government credit program, and taxation.
Government bonds are described, and local public
finance is explained, along with a treatment of
the relation between local and national public
finance.

425. Suzuki, Yoshio, ed. Financial Innovation and
Monetary Policy: Asia and the West. Asia and the
West: Proceedings of the 2nd International
Conference Held May 29-31, 1985 at the Bank of
Japan. Tokyo: University of Tokyo (Distributed by

Columbia University Press, New York), 1986.

This volume studies the changes in the financial structures of nations in Asia and the West due to the advent of computers, to changes in social and economic conditions, and to reactions to obsolescent financial regulations. Innovation in financing is seen as a spur to progress. The goals of price stability and continued growth are assessed. Topics include background discussions, deregulation possibilities, and monetary policy.

426. Suzuki, Yoshio. <u>Money and Banking in Contemporary Japan: The Theoretical Setting and Its Application</u>. Trans. John G. Greenwood. New Haven: Yale University Press, 1980.

Written with the view that theoretical accounts of monetary economics should attempt to encompass the various national banking systems and their workings, this important textbook examines Japan's monetary system The characteristics of Japan's financial structure are described, including the role of overloan and overborrowing, for example, as well as the investment-led policies and the artificially low interest-rate policies. The general equilibrium model of money and banking is outlined as it pertains to Japan. The theory and practice of bank behavior in Japan is presented, and consumer and corporate behaviors are also considered. The monetary instruments which bring policies into effect are described, including the monetary stabilization methods in the monetary market, loan policy and central bank practices. The effectiveness and future prospects of the Japanese banking system are assessed.

427. Suzuki, Yoshio. <u>Money, Finance, and Macroeconomic Performance in Japan</u>. Trans. Robert Alan Feldman. New Haven: Yale University Press, 1986.

Focusing on the period since 1973, this book analyzes the changes in Japan's monetary and financial system and monetary macroeconomic performance. Consisting of two parts, the books begins with the evolution of the financial system, covering the historical background for recent structural modifications. Statistical analysis reveals a decline in private financial intermediaries, a force leading to financial deregulation and reform. Financial innovation is also viewed from an international perspective. Part I closes with a look at the implications of these financial developments for the effectiveness of monetary policy. Part II deals with money and macroeconomic performance. It covers recent

Japanese inflation debates, the degree of success
of price stabilization policies, and explanations
for Japan´s recovery from the first oil price
shock. Theoretical and empirical analyses of yen
exchange rate movements are presented since the
1973 transition to a floating rate system. The
book concludes by focusing on monetary control by
the Bank of Japan, emphasizing an international
perspective.

428. United States. Congress. Joint Economic Committee.
The Japanese Financial System in Comparative
Perspective. Washington, D. C.: U. S. Government
Printing Office, 1982.

This essay attempts to counter some of the
prevailing views on the control of Japanese
finances by a conservative coalition of
politicians bureaucrats and big business. It
offers a description of the interaction of the
financial markets and the nonfinancial economy.
The Japanese system and the American are compared.
The evolution of the two countries, whether
tending toward convergence or divergence, is
explored. And the role of government is
identified as a structural determinant of markets,
even under control-free regimes. Analysis of the
government´s role in intermediation in the
financial system is undertaken. A contrast of the
Japanese and American economies is given.
Evolution of postwar financial structures is
traced, and policies are assessed.

429. Wade, Robert. "East Asian Financial Systems as a
Challenge to Economics: Lessons from Taiwan."
California Management Review. 27.4 (Summer
1985): 106-127.

A strong relationship between a rigid financial
system and successful industrialization has been
demonstrated in South Korea, Japan, and Taiwan.
This is contrary to conventional Western economic
theory. Rigid central control of the financial
system has benefitted these countries by: 1)
promoting a high rate of savings for financing
domestic industry by controlling the international
flow of capital, 2) reducing financial instability
in rapid growth companies with high debt/equity
ratios, 3) controlling credit allocation to aid
the development of selected industries, and 4)
receiving political support and cooperation from
the business community. Public sector financial
control has allowed these countries to create
successful industrial policies.

430. Yao, Jiro, ed. Monetary Factors in Japanese

Economic Growth. Kobe: Research Institute for
Economic and Business Administration, Kobe
University, 1970.

The main purpose of this book is to investigate
the monetary-fiscal aspects in the process of
Japanese economic growth and to find the
interrelations between the monetary and the real
factors. Essays cover topics such as economic
growth and monetary policy, supply of funds for
economic growth, investment behavior, "over-loan"
of commerical banks, foreign exchange reserves,
overseas investments and exports, and economic
instability tendencies. Monetary and fiscal
policies are explored.

431. Yasumoto, Dennis T. Japan and the Asian
     Development Bank. Studies of the East Asian
     Institute, Columbia University. New York: Praeger
     Publishing Co., 1983.

     In a report on the development and the role of the
     Asian Development Bank since its founding, this
     book provides a detailed history. The political
     and personal interplay of forces which shaped the
     bank are described. The interactions between
     Japan and neighboring countries are recounted.
     Japan's constructive leadership in the region
     emerges. There is significant attention paid to
     the staffing problems of the bank.

VII. MANAGEMENT, INDUSTRIAL ORGANIZATION, AND THE FIRM

Japanese management style, practices, and strategies are covered in this chapter. Corporate structure is discussed, along with the decision making process. United States responses to Japanese managerial methods are included. Material has also been added on industrial organization, industrial dualism, and anti-monopoly policy.

432. Abegglen, James C. The Japanese Factory: Aspects of its Social Organization. Center for International Studies, M.I.T. Glencoe, Ill.: Free Press, 1958.

Many observations of the Japanese factory comprise this study which is written in the belief that culture and tradition play an important role in the economics of the country. The large factory, employing more than 1,000 persons, is the emphasis here. Because there is a significant trend toward the development of heavy industry in the Asian region for the future, this concentration on the large factory is deliberate. But the study will not produce a formula for replication in, say, other Asian nations, because each country has its own special development. Ethnocentrism, which has hindered relations between the East and West, can be combatted by presenting more information to the technocrats and managers who are America's "ambassadors" to the East. Topics such as the terms of employment, rank and incentives, the place of work in the employees' life, and productivity are discussed.

433. Abegglen, James C. Management & Worker: The Japanese Solution. Tokyo: Sophia University, 1973.

This book updates the author's earlier, The Japanese Factory, which is reprinted here in part. New aspects of the study are updates on the Japanese scene in the 60's and 70's. There has been considerable debate aroused by the publication of the original version, in which the author gave a large measure of importance to the

large factory, and has been charged with
overlooking the role of the small ones.
Recruitment, distribution and training of the
labor force is covered. Treatment is also given
to the stability of labor relations and the new
technologies that are cropping up. Problems with
labor's lack of mobility and with international
management are also introduced.

434. Abegglen, James C. The Strategy of Japanese
     Business. Cambridge, Mass.: Ballinger, 1984.

This collection of essays and speeches by the
author covers four aspects of Japanese business
and economy: foreign trade, management, direct
foreign investment, and research and development.
In less than three decades, Japan has undergone a
period of rapid industrialization now producing
10% of world output. This is a point of departure
for modern history dominated by Western countries.
The Japanese have created their own economic
system distinct from the Soviet-type planned
economy and the American-type free economy. It is
economically sound and rational. The Japanese
firm is a communal organization that has
successfully separated ownership from control and
management, dissolving the conflict between
management and labor. Their management system has
its limits, but it flourishes in an environment of
high savings, capital abundance, a motivated labor
force, and good government-business relations.
Japan's industrial policy must be understood in
its own context and does not fit into a Western
paradigm. The government is neither the origin of
command nor an adversary of private business. It
is small, efficient, and development orientated
with a wide consensus between government and
business on national, international, and industry
issues. Japan is becoming more involved in direct
foreign investment and the internationalization of
its economy. Japan's R&D efforts are striving to
catch up in biogenetics, aerospace, atomic energy,
and ocean-resource development.

435. Abegglen, James C., and William V. Rapp.
     "Japanese Managerial Behavior and `Excessive
     Competition'." The Developing Economies. 8.4
     (Dec. 1970): 427-444.

It is argued that a number of aspects of Japanese
corporate behavior, including most basically long
experience with rapid growth, and also financial
and personnel policies as well as the cost effects
of growth, make maintenance of market share a
critical objective of Japanese management. This
overriding preoccupation with the maintenance and

expansion of market share is entirely realistic.
But a major consequence of this concern is the
degree of preemptive capital investment and
pricing that is termed "excessive competition."
The critical area of pricing behavior is discussed
as a successful means of translating into faster
growth. As economic development proceeds,
however, this management system may be called into
question in Japan.

436. Abegglen, James C., and George Stalk. Kaisha, the
Japanese Corporation: The New Competitors in World
Business. New York: Basic Books, 1985.

This book offers a detailed study of the internal
workings and structure of the Japanese
corporation. The role of the government, the
banks, and management is reconstructed, and the
part played by employee-management relations, the
external environment, and foreign influences is
described. The behavior and decision-making
patterns that the kaisha have followed in
regenerating the economy are uncovered. The
successful strategies that have led to the
expansion of the Japanese market share in so many
industries are analyzed. The technological drive
that motored much of the development is discussed,
with the role of the government. Financial
conditions and multinational ventures are
reviewed, and the future prospects are outlined.

437. Adams, Thomas F. M., and N. Kobayashi. World of
Japanese Business. Tokyo: Kodansha International
Ltd., 1969.

This book is a treatment of the interface between
Japan and the West, discussing the features of
Japanese culture which figure most prominently in
the exchange. The industrial basis of Japan, the
structure of business, and the decision-making
process in Japanese business are described. There
is a discussion of the Westerner's problems in
relating to the Japanese businessman. General
discussion is given of the growth, the
bureaucracy, and the system of marketing and
distribution in Japan. Comments are also offered
from the Japanese perspective about capital
liberalization, joint ventures, and management in
Japan.

438. Asian Regional Conferences on Industrial
Relations. Industrial Policies, Foreign
Investment and Labor in Asian Countries. Tokyo:
Japan Institute of Labour, 1978.

This volume contains the proceedings of the 7th

Conference entitled Asian Regional Conference on Industrial Relations, held in Tokyo in 1977. Its general areas of concern include the recent developments in the foreign investment sphere, as well as the labor situation in various Asian countries.

439. Bilgin, B. "Japan's Changing Industrial Strategy and Its Implications for Japanese Investment in Canada." Pacific Affairs: An International Review of Asia and the Pacific. 55.2 (Summer 1982): 267-272.

This article discusses reforms in the industrial structure of Japan and traces its impact of Japan's import and export trade patterns. A forecast is made to what extent Canada will benefit form the anticipated growth in Japanese foreign direct investments and capital joint-ventures. Statistics are given for 1965-1985.

440. Broadbridge, Seymour. Industrial Dualism in Japan: A Problem of Economic Growth & Structural Change. Chicago: Aldine, 1966.

The Japanese system is characterised as "dualistic" in the sense that very large corporations coexist with very small ones. These different sized companies permit very large differentials in wages to continue. The dualism in Japan is seen as a product of its origins, as Japan began to industrialize under the influence of advanced Western capitalism. Postwar pressures also contributed to its persistence. Economic growth in Japan is traced, and wage differentials are detailed. The difficulties which maintenance of Japanese dualism entails are many. The relationships among the small firms and between the small and the large are discussed, and the future of the small firm in Japan is considered.

441. Burks, Ardath W. Japan: Profile of a Postindustrial Power. Boulder, Co.: Westview Press, 1981.

This book gives an overview of Japan. It describes the landscape and the people, investigates Japanese tradition, and outlines the process of modern industrialization. Japanese culture and postwar politics are described. Basic features of the economy are examined, and the postindustrial characteristics of Japan are outlined. This is a society in which generalized wealth creates a broad consensus and mutes political-economic discord.

442. Caves, Richard E., and Masu Uekusa. <u>Industrial</u>
     <u>Organization in Japan</u>. Washington, D.C.:
     Brookings Institution, 1976.

     Economic analysis and statistical methods are used
     to examine the structure of Japanese business and
     industry. Extensive comparisons have been made
     between Japanese and American industrial systems.
     The study finds similiar economic forces working
     in both countries and notes that Japan´s
     industrial policy is a rolling comprise between
     shifting goals of public policy and the economic
     interests of the industrial sectors. Japan has a
     number of distinctive industrial features:
     industrial groups, the practice of permanent
     employment, the prevalence of small businesses,
     and other. The structure of Japanese markets and
     patterns of competition differ significantly from
     the U.S. In addition, environmental influences on
     industrial organization, mergers, company finance
     and capital markets are discussed. Allocative and
     technical efficiencies are studied along with
     imported technology and industrial progress.

443. Clark, Rodney. <u>The Japanese Company</u>. New Haven,
     Conn.: Yale University Press, 1979.

     This book presents a general overview of the
     Japanese company, how it runs, how it affects
     those working for it, and how it influences
     Japanese society. Focus is first centered on the
     present position of the company in Japanese
     society with a brief historical account. Its
     organization, management, and methods of selecting
     managers and their tasks are covered with a
     comparative look at American companies. Next the
     labor market is considered, explaining how people
     join and leave companies, how far "life
     employment" exists, and how the labor market and
     company policies affect society in general. The
     aging of the work force forms a source of
     potential change. The quality of the relationship
     between company and employees is analyzed.
     Lastly, the influence of companies on Japanese
     society are given with a discussion of the
     possibility of change.

444. Dimock, Marshall E. <u>Japanese Technocracy:</u>
     <u>Management and Government in Japan</u>. New York:
     Walker/Weatherhill, 1968.

     The governing process in Japan is systematically
     treated, with the total context of Japanese
     culture as the starting point. Many factors are
     identified, including the actions of pressure
     groups, the civil bureaucracy´s role, and the

departmentalism of the government. The power of
public corporations and the status of universities
are also assessed. The climate of
cosmopolitanism, and the changing world situation
are also examined. The future for Japanese
progress is assessed.

445. Dreyfack, Raymond. Making It in Management, the
Japanese Way. Rockville Centre, N.Y.: Farnsworth
Publishing Co., 1982.

The management philosophy in the U.S. is not
adequate for the success of U.S. business. On the
other hand, the Japanese have many points to offer
the U.S. There is an appreciation of the
importance of the people who work in Japanese
industry, and a tendency to operate by consensus.
There are specific descriptions of Japanese
companies which demonstrate the Japanese
methodology. U.S. practices are also discussed.
Productivity problems in the U.S. are identified
and changes in attitude are recommended.

446. Fields, George. From Bonsai to Levi´s. New York:
Macmillan, 1983.

This book is offered as a report on the Japanese
society from the point of view of the manager of
one of Japan´s consumer research firms. It
describes the personality and traditions of the
people with many anecdotes and original insights.
Without the use of a preconceived theory, the book
provides useful and genuine information for a
sketch of the people who make up Japanese society
today.

447. Haitani, Kanji. The Japanese Economic System: An
Institutional Overview. Lexington, Mass.:
Lexington Books, D.C. Heath and Co., 1976.

With the goal of telling how the Japanese economic
system is organized, this book describes
institutions, with a stress on the economic and
some reference to political and social
institutions. The important role of group
relations and loyalties is identified. Rank and
status are described, and the effects of the
respect for rank on individual freedom, dignity
and creativity are examined. The behavior of
institutions is delineated in education, the
bureaucracy, public works, business and industrial
organization, labor, and the monetary and fiscal
field.

448. Iyori, Horishi. Anti-Monopoly Legislation in
Japan. New York: Federal Legal Publication, 1969.

This book discusses the theory and practice of
anti-monopoly legislation in Japan. A general
history is provided of the development of
industrial trusts and the government´s relation to
them.

449. Japan. Chusho Kigyocho. Outline of Major Measures
for Small and Medium Enterprises in Japan. Tokyo:
Small and Medium Enterprise Agency, MITI, 1972.

A MITI report outlining the government´s
industrial policy for the development and
promotion of small and medium sized enterprises.

450. Japan. Chusho Kigyocho. Present Aspect of
Measures for Small and Medium Enterprises in
Japan. Tokyo: Small and Medium Enterprise
Agency, MITI, 1970.

A 1970 MITI report is presented. It deals with
the current policies affecting the development of
small business in Japan and the government´s
efforts to promote it.

451. Kagono, Tadao, et al. Strategic Vs. Evolutionary
Management: A U.S.-Japan Comparison of Strategy
and Organization. Advanced Series in Management
10. Amsterdam: Elsevier Science Pub. Co., 1985.

Variant Title: U.S.-Japan Comparison of Strategy
and Organization: Strategic Versus Evolutionary
Management.

This is the product of a research project which
began in 1976. The authors conducted an extensive
survey of American and Japanese corporations, to
make comparisons about the actual management
practices of the two countries. Data is presented
and analyzed. The Japanese management approach is
labelled the "operations orientation," and the
U.S. approach the "production orientation."
Another comparison resulted in a characterization
of Japanese organization patterns as "group" and
U.S. patterns as "bureaucratic." The methodology
used for the research was that of an open
engineering view of organizations. However,
during the project, findings that could not be
explained in this method were encountered, and a
new, evolutionary view of organizations was
developed.

452. Kono, Toyohiro. Strategy and Structure of
Japanese Enterprises. Armonk, N.Y.: M.E. Sharpe,
1984.

The strategy, structure and strategic decisions

involved in Japanese industrial management are
analyzed. Top management, goals of the
organization, product-market strategy, capability
structure, and operations are examined. The
decision-making process is reviewed. For each
sub-system, models of the relationships are
offered. Each set of relations affects others.
Research is presented on 102 large manufacturing
corporations that are relatively successful.
Similarities and differencies with practices in
other countries are pointed out. Many of the
universal characteristics of management in Japan
are identified.

453. Lee, Sang M., and Gary Schwendiman, eds. Japanese
Management: Cultural and Environmental
Considerations. New York: Praeger Publishers,
1982.

While the well known management by information
style of management has been followed because of
its reliance on short-term objectives and top-down
decision-making, the new concept of management by
ideology is a better characterization of the
process used in Japan. There is more top-down and
bottom-up communication, consensus decision-making
and commitment to the organization. Questions
about what can be learned from the Japanese, the
socio-cultural aspects, the management environment
in Japan, and Japan-U.S. relations are raised.

454. Marsh, Robert M., and Hiroshi Mannari.
Modernization and the Japanese Factory.
Princeton: Princeton University Press, 1976.

In a study which uses in-depth ethnographic
descriptions of three firms and cross firm
comparisons, it is argued that the paternalism-
lifetime commitment model of Japanese factories
exaggerates their "Japaneseness." Most successful
firms have moved away from traditionalism and
toward more modern structures. Firms which do not
modernize, it is predicted, will show signs of
strain. Although a firm may show a given feature
of the paternalism-lifetime commitment model, the
empirical consequences of that attribute predicted
by the model are often not observed in the data.
Finally, the more "Japanese" characteristics of
organization have less impact on the functioning
of firms than the more universal organizational
features.

455. Matsushita, Konosuke. Japan at the Brink. Trans.
Charles S. Terry. Tokyo: Kodansha International,
1976.

This book discusses the economic recessions in the
mid 1970´s and sees grave management problems
emerging for Japan. The government is in
confusion, there is tight money and a deep
economic slump. Issues such as the oil crisis,
inflation, and lack of self reliance are raised.
Dissatisfaction of the Japanese youth is
described. Democracy has been misunderstood in
Japan, it is argued, and political commentary is
offered. Educational issues and price stability
through legislation are discussed.

456. McMillan, Charles J. The Japanese Industrial
     System. 2nd ed. De Gruyter Studies in
     Organization 1. Berlin & New York: W. de Gruyter,
     1985 (1st edition 1984).

     A theoretical understanding of Japan´s economic
     success is sought. The book attempts to integrate
     the various factors -- managerial efficiency,
     production orientation, government-business
     relations, innovation, industrial planning, and
     others into a unified whole by means of management
     and organization theories. A model is constructed
     around "hardware" and "software" technologies at
     the macro and micro levels. Macro hardware
     consists of taxes, investments, science, and
     energy policies; micro hardware includes
     automation, plant and equipment, computerization,
     and energy utilization. Macro software
     encompasses business-government relations,
     industry associations, management-labor relations,
     ideologies, and values; micro software refers to
     employment practices, decision making, information
     diffusion, and social innovation. Topics covered
     include business-government relations, industrial
     planning, technology and knowledge
     intensification, education and management
     recruitment, management strategy and organization,
     human resource strategies, production and
     operations management, marketing, Japanese
     management abroad, money and banking, and future
     prospects. The Japanese industrial system works
     so well because there is a skillful combination of
     hardware and software technologies at the
     national, industrial and firms levels maximizing
     their collective effort.

457. Monroe, Wilbur F., and Eisuke Sakakibara. The
     Japanese Industrial Society: Its Organizational,
     Cultural, and Economic Underpinnings. Austin:
     Bureau of Business Research, University of Texas
     at Austin, 1977.

     This monograph presents an analysis of the
     management of the postwar Japanese economy,

integrating social and cultural factors with
traditional economic analysis. A broad
analytical framework is developed to examine
noneconomic factors which played an important part
in Japan's national life. Various noneconomic
factors studied include the Japanese sense of
"mutual dependence", organizational "verticalism",
lifelong employment and seniority systems, and the
Japanese educational system. The economic
analysis is placed in its historical context,
concentrating on those factors which contributed
to Japan's spectacular rate of growth.

458. Morse, Ronald A., ed. The Politics of Japan's
     Energy Strategy: Resources-Diplomacy-Security.
     Research Papers and Policy Studies 3. Berkeley,
     Calif.: University of California, Berkeley;
     Institute of East Asian Studies, 1981.

     There is a link between international military and
     trade issues, domestic Japanese politics and
     bureaucratic structure, and management actions of
     the Japanese regarding their energy policies.
     While the stereotype indicates a perfect
     coordination between Japan's corporations, banks
     and Ministry of International Trade and Industry,
     in many ways this picture is inaccurate. There
     has been turmoil in the oil supply situation, and
     many points of friction between the U.S. and
     Japan, competitors now in the oil supply markets.
     Interaction between the U.S. and Japan on the
     nuclear technology front, and on energy research,
     has been difficult at times. This book is
     dedicated to issues of Japanese energy policies,
     strategies, and aims. The chapters are revised
     papers presented at the annual convention of the
     Association of Asian Studies, held in Toronto,
     Canada, in March 1981.

459. Mutoh, Hiromichi. Development in the Japan's
     Industrial Structure Since Oil-Crisis. Japan
     Economic Research Center Paper 33. Tokyo: Japan
     Economic Research Center, 1980.

     The object of this study is to bring to the
     forefront the strengths and weaknesses of Japan's
     economic structure. Indicators for the various
     industrial sectors are tracked for the years 1960-
     1977, including value-added, employment, labor
     productivity, prices, plant and equipment
     investment, exports and imports, and finally the
     consumption structure of households. There is a
     comparison of various industries offered. The
     context of the study is the post-oil-crisis
     period, primarily the years from 1973 through
     1977. The work was produced on consignment to the

Commission of the European Communities.

460. Niino, K. "Dilemmas of Anti-Monopoly Policy in Japan." Kobe University Economic Review. 21 (1975): 1-8.

This article discussed the reasons why the proposed revision of the Anti-Monopoly Act did not succeed. A brief history of anti-monopoly legislation since 1947 is given. A description is provided of changes in the economic structure occurring in the 1970's. It appears that the fundamental dilemma of industrial policy is reconciling the conflict between specific steering policy aims and anti-monopoly policy as an industrial order policy.

461. Odaka, Kunio. Toward Industrial Democracy: Management and the Workers in Modern Japan. East Asian Monographs 80. Cambridge: Harvard University Press, 1975.

This book offers a view of the managerial ideology of Japan, and the current trends toward more democratic systems. A critique of prevalent theories of Japan's management patterns is given. Data are presented covering Japanese workers' attitudes and working conditions. The importance of the opportunity to innovate at the workplace and of the role of leisure time is assessed. The workers' identification with companies and unions is evaluated, and their attitudes toward work and leisure are described. From this data, some programmatic measures are suggested which would further democratize the Japanese management system. Some of these ideas have been presented in other forums.

462. Ohmae, Kenichi. The Mind of the Strategist: The Art of Japanese Business. New York: McGraw-Hill Book Co., 1982.

Japanese business acumen is treated from the point of view of an experienced business strategist. The competitive state of mind is described as a natural talent or intuition. Too much rationality inhibits the bold innovative flair that a real strategist must exhibit. Sample problems are examined, and key factors for success are identified. Building on relative superiority and pursuing aggressive initiatives are outlined. Corporate strategies and decision making are assessed.

463. Olsen, Edward A. Japan: Economic Growth, Resource Scarcity, and Environmental Constraints. Boulder,

Co.: Westview Press, 1978.

This work focuses on Japan as a nation which must
face neo-Malthusean limits to its resources, or
run into a catastrophe. Because so many modern
resources are non-renewable, economic and
political management must be directed at the
management of these resources, particularly in
Japan. An overview of Japanese economic growth is
offered. Changing Japanese view of nature are
explored, along with society's constraints. The
neo-Malthusian prospects for Japan as it must
confront scarcity in relation to its growing
population are traced. Internationalism, economic
vulnerability of Japan, and Japan's policy options
are explored, including non-action, territorial
expansionism, negotiated self-sufficiency, and
cooperation.

464. Ouchi, William G. The M-Form Society: How
American Teamwork Can Capture the Competitive
Edge. Reading, Mass.: Addison-Wesley, 1984.

A study of the lessons to be derived from business
organizations and applied to the problems of
managing society. "M-form" organizations are
those that are multidivisional. By in-depth
research, an attempt is made to understand methods
of developing a government-business teamwork
relation without giving up freedoms and ways to
improve the quality of this cooperative effort. A
database is provided as a framework for teamwork
analysis, as well as presenting an extensive case-
study type of approach. An agenda is presented
for transforming American society and rebuilding
international competitiveness.

465. Ouchi, William G. Theory Z: How American Business
Can Meet the Japanese Challenge. Reading, Mass.:
Addison-Wesley Publishing Co., 1981.

This book addresses the practicalities of applying
an understanding of Japanese management to
American business. While some aspects of the
Japanese system are purely cultural and cannot be
transported elsewhere, there are essential
components of the method which pertain to the
solution of business problems that are being faced
in similar ways in the U.S. Theory Z suggest that
involved workers are the answer to the question of
increasing productivity. Trust and subtlety, as
well as intimacy, are social factors that build
the involvement of workers. A comparison of
Japanese and American firms is offered, with a
blueprint for change in the U.S.

466. Pegels, Carl. _Japan vs. the West: Implications for Management_. Hingham, Mass.: KNP (Distributed by Kluwer Boston, Inc.), 1984.

On the belief that Japan´s successful management of its economy is a product of its methods and these methods are replicable in other countries, the Japanese production management system is analyzed. A detailed comparison is made between Japanese industry and Western industry. Key practices such as the focus of factories, the supplier´s integration with the process, and participation style of management are outlined. The system as it is actually operated by the Japanese comes under discussion, with the view that Japanese culture is not of itself a key ingredient in Japan´s success. The extent of Japanese style management´s penetration into Western economies is considered, and there is also an examination of future prospects.

467. Rau, S. K. _Rural Industrialization: Policy and Programmes in Four Asian Countries_. Tokyo: Asian Productivity Organization, 1985.

This is a comparative report on the cottage industries in four Asian countries: India, Philippines, South Korea, and Japan. It describes the structure and development of cottage industries in each country and government policy towards them.

468. Sasaki, Naoto. _Management and Industrial Structure in Japan_. Oxford: Pergamon Press, 1981.

This book is an examination of the entrepreneurial aspects of Japanese industrial growth. Cultural and economic background of Japanese management is given, with reference to the closed nature of the society and the dualism of its corporate structure, which includes both the very large and the very small firms. There is a detailed analysis of the management of human resources and its decision making mechanism. Policy coordination among industries and government is discussed, including specific cross-industry cooperation. There is also a treatment of the changing international environment and its impact on Japanese management. Japanese management in turn has an impact on other nations. One example is the present "retirement age revolution" in which senior managers call into question the lifetime employment assumptions held to be absolute by many in Japan. Many other cultural changes will lead to challenging new problems for the Japanese in the future.

469. Saso, Mary, and Stuart Kirby. Japanese Industrial
     Competition to 1990. Economist Intelligence Unit
     Special Series 1. Cambridge, Mass.: Abt Books,
     1982.

     This book consists of two reports. The first
     deals with Japanese industry. It begins by
     covering the structure of a typical Japanese
     manufacturing companies: capital structure,
     managerial systems, labor conditions, small and
     medium-sized firms, and the role of general
     trading companies. A review is provided of
     Japan's economic performance for the years 1960-
     1980. Further chapters include competing and
     cooperating with Japanese enterprises, ending with
     an overview of future developments in Japanese
     industry. The second part turns to Japan's role
     in the 1980's. It presents a picture of Japan's
     energy scene and its alternatives, a description
     of the economic base for Japan's development, and
     attitudes toward work and leisure. Perspectives
     on future trends in patterns of trade, economic
     growth, and trade imbalances are given.
     Projections are offered to 1990, including such
     areas as inflation, official policy, technological
     change, R&D, raw materials, and external
     relations.

470. Sato, Kazuo, ed. Industry and Business in Japan.
     London: Croom Helm, 1980.

     A compendium of essays by Japan's foremost writers
     on Japanese industrial organization, this book
     consists of twelve essays. The theme of the book
     is an evaluation of the concept of "Japan, Inc."
     The force of Japan's great progress with the
     support of the government has attracted many
     studies from within Japan. Historical views of
     the industrial organization in Japan are given.
     Particular industry studies are offered, in
     particular detailing the auto industry and iron
     and steel. The nature of the various business
     groups is analyzed, and an evaluation of the
     industrial policy and its role in recent growth is
     offered. There are surveys of industry studies
     since 1960.

471. Sato, Kazuo, and Yasuo Hoshino, eds. The Anatomy
     of Japanese Business. Armonk, N.Y.: M.E. Sharpe,
     Inc., 1984.

     A collection of essays written by Japanese experts
     on Japanese management and business practices. A
     comparison of American and Japanese management
     contrasts them as mechanistic vs. organic systems.
     An empirical study of the relation between chief

executives and firm growth is given. Also
analyzed is the strcuture of management control
and ownership, along with interfirm relations in
enterprise grouping. Case studies are provided
for Toyota´s and Fuji´s production systems. Other
essays cover the grand strategy of Japanese
business, diversification strategy and economic
performance, and a comparison of the financial
characteristics between merging and non-merging
firms.

472. Schonberger, Richard J. Japanese Manufacturing
     Techniques: Nine Hidden Lessons in Simplicity.
     New York: Free Press, Division of Macmillan
     Publishing Co., 1982.

     This book distills the essential principles from
     Japanese management practice, beginning with the
     idea that these lessons can be taken up by other
     countries. First, elimination of excess
     inventories and staff is discussed. Quality
     control and plant configurations are presented.
     Flexible production line management and purchasing
     are described. Use of self-improvement and less
     specialist intervention are examined. The
     prospect for the U.S. to adopt such natural,
     simple proposals is assessed.

473. Sethi, S. Prakash. Japanese Business and Social
     Conflict: A Comparative Analysis of Response
     Patterns with American Business. Special
     Publication of the Institute of Business and
     Economic Research, University of California,
     Berkeley. Cambridge, Mass.: Ballinger Publishing
     Co., 1975.

     The remarkable economic growth in Japan can be
     attributed to a strategic combination of premodern
     and modern factors. An analytic framework for
     understanding corporate behavior in Japan is
     offered. Traditional society is described, with
     attention to its norms. Management and issues of
     public concern relating to the environment and
     consumer problems are outlined. The tactical
     responses of business to social problems are
     analyzed, and conclusions are offered about the
     prospects for the future.

474. Shinohara, Miyohei, and Douglas Fisher. The Role
     of Small Industry in the Process of Economic
     Growth: Japan, India. Bert F. Hoselitz, ed.
     Paris: Mouton, 1968.

     Giving an account of the small-scale industries in
     Japan and India, this work is divided into two
     parts. Mr. Shinohara´s survey of the Japanese

small industry is composed of assessment of the
firms with one to three employees and other small
firms with four employees or more. The nature of
such operations is examined, and there is a
treatment of companies with less than 100
employees. Because of the unique position of the
small scale industries, the question of why they
exist is addressed. The study is not intended as
a complete examination of their role vis a vis the
larger firms, however.

475. Taylor, Jared. Shadows of the Rising Sun: A
     Critical View of the "Japanese Miracle". New
     York: William Morrow and Co., 1983.

     This book offers a counterpoise to the tendency to
     portray Japan in exaggeratedly favorable terms. A
     realistic portrait of Japan must include a glimpse
     of what lies in the shadows of success, and those
     features may be differences from characteristics
     of the West, not necessarily failures. Another
     aim is to caution managers in America and Europe
     who hope to learn the business secrets of the East
     and apply them to problems back home. Some
     adaptations of corporate strategy to distinctive
     features of Japanese society may not work as well
     elsewhere. The first part of the book gives those
     elements of Japanese thinking that seem most
     different from Western ideas. The second part
     focuses on specific aspects of Japanese life.

476. Vogel, Ezra F., ed. Modern Japanese Organization
     and Decision-Making. Berkeley: University of
     California Press, 1975.

     Changes have been occuring in the consensus
     underlying Japanese organizational behavior. This
     collection seeks to refine and modify the concepts
     used in describing Japanese organization. Some
     popular notions have taken on exaggerated senses,
     such as "Japan, Inc." The idea of Japanese
     organizations' relying on documents drafted at
     lower levels is also explored. Groupism and long-
     range goal orientation are described. The concept
     of fair share as it appears in conflict resolution
     is examined. Bureaucratic elitism and cores of
     business leadership are presented.

477. Woronoff, Jon. Inside Japan Inc. Tokyo: Lotus
     Press, 1982.

     This book explores the inner management workings
     of the Japanese corporate system. Its smooth-
     running surface belies many problems underneath.
     The lifetime employment practices, the role of
     women, and disillusionment of workers are

considered.   Various defects in the system are
alluded to.

478. Yamanaka, Tokutaro, ed.   Small Business in Japan's
     Economic Progress.   Tokyo: Asahi Evening News,
     1971.

     There is a significant sector of small and medium
     scale business in Japan.   A range of topics
     relating to research on the history and
     development of medium and small-scale firms is
     offered.   Distinctive features of these companies
     are traced, along with attention to the financing,
     industrial relations, management, organization,
     and role of the sector as a whole.   The treatment
     of each theme is brief and succinct, as a cursory
     overview.

479. Yonekawa, Shinichi, and Hideki Yoshihara.
     Business History of General Trading Companies.
     The International Conference on Business History
     13.   Tokyo: University of Tokyo Press, 1987.

     These are essays which deal with management of the
     British, French, German, and Japanese merchant
     firms which specialize in international trade.   In
     Japan the general trading companies have a long
     history.   They were established under governmental
     initiative.   The course of events for various
     companies is traced.

480. Yoshino, Michael Y.   The Japanese Marketing
     System: Adaptations and Innovations.   Cambridge,
     Mass.: MIT Press, 1971.

     With the view that a nation's marketing system is
     influenced by the environment and also causes
     changes in the human needs of the people, this
     research investigates the effects of Japan's
     emergence as a high-consumption society.   The
     unique characteristics of Japan's new marketing
     system are identified, and the influence of the
     system on Japan's social system is examined.
     Changes in the market orientation, the
     distribution structure, and the traditional
     marketing institutions are described.   The role of
     finance and government is examined.   Recent
     developments and problems are noted.

VIII. PRODUCTIVITY AND LABOR RELATIONS

Topics contained in this chapter consist of labor mobility, permanent employment, productivity drives, methods of improving productivity, the labor market, unions, industrial relations, and their contributions toward economic growth.

481. Aoki, Masohiko, ed. Economic Analysis of the Japanese Firm. Contributions to Economic Analysis 151. New York: North-Holland (Distributed by Elsevier Science Publishing Co.), 1984.

These collected essays are written by economists from the U.S., Japan, U.K., and Israel. An economic analysis of the Japanese firm is sought which will provide a better understanding of their economy as a whole. Part I deals with the firm's internal organization and industrial relations, covering labor mobility and job tenure, the effects of trade unions on productivity, and the workings of the labor market. Part II discusses personal savings, the bonus payment system, corporate finance, and bank vs individual investments. Part III analyzes the firm's external relations including the economic role of financial corporate grouping, government intervention, ownership and financing of companies, and business groupings and government-industry relations. The book ends with Part IV examining Japanese managerial efficiency and motivation system.

482. Asher, S. M., and K. Inoue. "Industrial Manpower Development in Japan." Finance and Development. 22.3 (Sept. 1985): 23-26.

The Japanese approach to the development of manpower for its industry is discussed. The central government issues broad guidelines and perspectives which the schools, colleges, universities, and companies follow. These guidelines are based on information flowing in from all segments of the society. Comparative labor productivity in manufacturing is provided for Japan, Germany, and the United States. Also vocational training institutions and training

courses are described. Statistics are given for
1970-1978.

483. Asian Productivity Organization. Achievements in
the First Decade of the Productivity Drive in
Japan. Translation Series 7. Tokyo: Asian
Productivity Organization, 1968 (1965).

The Japanese productivity drive which began in
1954 is assessed. At a cost of about $28 million,
which came from U.S. sources and from funds raised
by the Japanese themselves, the program enabled
Japan to overtake even the advanced countries in
some areas of industry, to ride out several waves
of business adjustment, and to make spectacular
growth overall. Problems of structural change,
however, were encountered: bankruptcies in small
business, slumps in the stock market, and
diminution of corporate profits. This book covers
the main projects directed by the Japan
Productivity Center.

484. Asian Productivity Organization. APO. Japan
Productivity Center Tokyo: Asian Productivity
Organization, 1965-.

Monographs published under the titles, APO, Annual
Report, and Conference Report, and others, are
included. These consist of summaries of the
workshops, training seminars, conferences, and
reports each year on productivity in the Asian
region. Titles concerning Japan are authored by
the Japan Productivity Center. A partial list of
volumes not entered separately in the present work
includes: Economic Growth and the Productivity
Movement in Japan, 1973; Industrial Relations and
Productivity in Japan, 1971; Three Principles of
Productivity Movement in Japan, 1985.

485. Baumol, William J., and Kenneth McLennan, eds.
Productivity Growth and U.S. Competitiveness. A
Supplementary Paper of the Committee for Economic
Development. New York: Oxford University Press,
1985.

The nature of the productivity problem confronting
the United States is the focal point of this
collection of research papers. It summarizes the
results of empirical research investigating the
causes of a declining rate of productivity growth
in the 1960's in the U.S. and in other
industrialized countries several years later. An
comparative analysis is provide of the U.S. and
Japan. Evidence is given showing that Japan's
growth in total-factor productivity was comparable
to the U.S., while Japan's manufacturing labor

productivity grew almost three times faster. The
superior performance of the Japanese can be
attributed to their higher saving and investment
record. Two conclusions are drawn: that the
investment rate is the prime long-term contributor
to an increase in per capita income and standard
of living; and that productivity growth is a long-
run issue.

486. Burnham, John M. Japanese Productivity: A Study
     Mission Report. Falls Church, Va.: American
     Production and Inventory Control Society, 1983.

     An international group of business managers
     studies the Japanese system of inventory and
     production control. It contains statistics and
     descriptions of plants visited by the group, with
     observations about each company's management
     philosophy, strategy, engineering, human
     relations, and production and inventory
     management. Master scheduling, materials
     planning, material control, capacity planning, and
     inventory performance are discussed. Conclusions
     emphasize the cooperative spirit and the desire
     for continual improvements by each company.
     Emulation of the Japanese is encouraged.

487. Christiansen, Gregory B., and Jan S. Hogendorn.
     "Japanese Productivity: Adapting to Changing
     Comparative Advantage in the Face of Lifetime
     Employment Commitments." Quarterly Review of
     Economics & Business. 23.2 (Summer 1983): 23-39.

     The Japanese industrial policy actively pursues
     the reallocation of resources and labor from
     declining industries to expanding ones. At the
     same time, job security is guaranteed for a
     significant portion of the labor force. An
     explanation of how "lifetime employment" coincides
     with Japan's current industrial policy is
     explored. The role of the Japanese Ministry of
     International Trade and Industry, as a joint
     government-business effort to efficiently develop
     the economy is presented. Also an analysis of the
     myths and realities of lifetime employment and the
     role of "temporary" workers is detailed.

488. Cole, Robert E. Japanese Blue Collar: The
     Changing Tradition. Berkeley, Calif.: University
     of California Press, 1971.

     An empirical study of the blue-collar worker in
     Japan, this book attempts to dispel myths and
     identify the uniqueness of Japan's situation.
     Paternalism, rapid growth of industrialization,
     and culture have made important contributions.

The national legislative framework is described, and a picture is drawn of the worker´s situation. Wages, advancement, security, and unity among workers are discussed. The relations to the company and the union are explored. Changing characteristics are assessed.

489. Dore, Ronald P. Flexible Rigidities: Industrial Policy & Structural Adjustment in the Japanese Economy, 1970-1980. Stanford, Calif.: Stanford University Press, 1986.

The Japanese economy consists of union monopolies, cartels, and tied dealerships, all the things free marketers denounce as "rigidities." Normally, these "rigidities" are seen as preventing a smooth adjustment to disturbing economic forces. However, during the 1970´s international economic crises, the Japanese economy adjusted far better than the advanced Western economies. The author finds the answer in the flexibility of the Japanese industrial policy to handle these apparent structural and institutional difficulties. By focusing on the Japanese labor market, this study traces its impact on trade policy and practices. A detailed case study of the textile industry is presented. The success of Japan´s economic adjustments holds a lesson for the West, particularly Great Britain, in terms of efficiency, quality control, and international competitiveness.

490. Hall, Robert W. Driving the Productivity Machine: Production Planning and Control in Japan: A Research Report. Falls Church, Va.: American Production and Inventory Control Society, 1981.

Repetitive manufacturing consists of industrial processes which produce discrete units by the use of repetitive processes. The units flow through work centers which are arranged in the sequence in which operations take place. Balancing production rates at the work centers thus becomes very important. Management of the supply of units that is to be kept in inventory is also a key to success. This industry has many special needs in terms of the process control techniques it must use. Japanese practices are compared with American practices. The SEIBAN and KANBAN methods are described. Of particular interest are the methods for having the suppliers absorb the ups and downs in the production and distribution chain.

491. Hanami, Tadashi. Labor Relations in Japan Today. Tokyo: Kodansha International Ltd., 1979.

This book offers a discussion of the structure and operation of the Japanese industrial relations system since 1945. Conflicts are staged in a different way in Japan and unlike the overt disagreement which often reigns in the U.S., the Japanese handle conflict in more subtle ways. Nonetheless, conflicts are present, and once the normal cooperation between worker and manager ceases, there is often a highly charged and tense period of conflict marked by subtle emotional turns which can readily lead to violence. Personal relations, the legal background, and the nature of unionism in Japan are treated. The various types of labor disputes are categorized and described. Methods of settling the conflicts are examined.

492. Harari, Ehud. The Politics of Labor Legislation in Japan: National-International Interaction. Berkeley: University of California Press, 1973.

This book traces the interaction of Japanese political forces in response to the Japanese unions´ complaints about their restricted freedom to organize. For a nine year period, from 1957-66, the unions carried on a highly political campaign with the support of the International Labor Organization, which centered around the complaints that Japan´s laws unfairly restricted the membership of public sector unions and that there was police interference in union affairs. This dispute was solved with considerable flexibility shown by the Japanese government. The background and the forces which enabled this conflict to be played out are explored. Explanations of the process are offered.

493. Hirono, Ryokichi. Factors which Hinder or Help Productivity Improvement in the Asian Region: A Review and the Prospect-- National Report-- Japan. Tokyo: Asian Productivity Organization, 1980.

This study was intended to address the question of national efforts in productivity enhancement in Japan. A recapitulation of the economic performance of Japan during the 1960´s and 70´s is given. Growth patterns in output and employment are traced. Selected industries are discussed, including heavy and chemical, light, and technology-intensive industries with regard to the factors which affect the productivity of each. Demand, competition, industrial policy, political stability, capital intensity, technology and industrial relations are topics that are considered.

494. Inoue, Ken. The Education and Training of
     Industrial Manpower in Japan. World Bank Staff
     Working Papers 729. Washington, D.C.: World Bank,
     1985.

     Written by a consultant to the World Bank, this
     book describes the education and training process
     that has been used to transform the agrarian
     society of Japan into a leading industrial nation.
     History is presented since 1880, with a focus on
     the modern period. The formation of manpower is
     recounted through a discussion of schools and
     training institutes. The utilization of manpower
     is examined through the role of the business
     community. There are recommendations offered for
     the developing countries from the Japanese
     experience.

495. Japan Economic Research Center. The Japanese
     Labor Market in 1990: Changes in the Industrial
     Structure and Employment Problems. Tokyo: Japan
     Economic Research Center, 1978.

     This book is a compendium of forecasts which deals
     with the labor and industrial structure issues in
     the Japanese economy. Predictions are based on
     current statistics and trends.

496. Japan Institute of Labor. Employment and
     Employment Policy. Japanese Industrial Relation
     Series 1. Tokyo: Japan Institute of Labor, 1982.

     In this report an analysis is given of Japanese
     manpower policies and conditions affecting labor
     supply. The changing industrial structure,
     increased emphasis on high-tech research and
     development, and the aging of the labor force are
     some of the factors influencing the future course
     of industrial relations and employment policies.
     Projections are made trends in the labor supply.

497. Japan Productivity Center. Measuring
     Productivity: Trends and Comparisons from the
     First International Productivity Symposium. New
     York: UNIPUB, 1984.

     The concepts involved in the measurement of
     productivity are examined. Fluctuations in growth
     and the problems in using various economic
     indicators are discussed. Terms such as
     "efficiency" and "real" are analyzed. The
     difficulty with sorting out the net and gross
     productivity measures is examined. Specific
     topics discussed include white collar
     productivity, total factor productivity, capital
     input measurement difficulties, international

comparisons, and Japanese growth in productivity
overall with an econometric view.

498. Kaneko, Yoshio. "Employment and Wages." The
Developing Economies. 8.4 (Dec. 1970): 445-474.

The sharp increase in educated workers has been
accomodated by the postwar economic growth in
technological sectors. Labor unions with left-
wing ideology have been well harmonized within
enterprises. Wages have been increasing faster
after 1965, with a new increase in household
expenditures. This tends to push for further wage
increases, which have been met through the
favorable balance of payments situation.
Production as a priority has however created
increasingly important problems of public hazards,
pollution, and an underdeveloped state of social
overhead capital. Some questions for the future
are raised.

499. Kawasaki, Asuo. Changes in Japan's Labour Market
During High-Rate Economic Growth. Productivity
Series 9. Tokyo: Asian Productivity Organization;
UNIPUB, 1975.

This book focuses on the changes in labor supply
conditions, especially during the period of very
rapid economic growth. Labor supply and labor
relations are treated. The relation between
government and industry is explored. This volume
is one of the Asian Productivity Organization
monographs.

500. Levine, Solomon B. Industrial Relations in
Postwar Japan. Urbana, Ill.: University of
Illinois Press, 1958.

The marked impact of the U.S. occupation of Japan
after the war is shown in the labor management
system's recent changes. These reforms condition
the entire system, from its managerial style, to
its trade-union movement. The philosophy of trade
unions, as well as the nature of collective
bargaining and conflict, must be seen in this
context. The government regulation of industrial
relations has been influencing the labor-
management system through the level of benefits
and wages which can be set, and through other
mechanisms.

501. Levine, Solomon B., and Hisashi Kawada. Human
Resources in Japanese Industrial Development.
Princeton, N.J.: Princeton University Press, 1980.

The process by which Japan has marshalled its

human resources is explored, primarily emphasizing
the large scale industries. Historical contexts
are described, through which the generation of
industrial skill became possible. Education,
human resource strategy, and the management of
tradition are important factors for the Japanese
case. The work force and its talents, whether
underutilized or not, become factors in the
dynamic change in a society that is modernizing.
Long term strategy and particularism, the factors
unique to Japan, are assessed. Values of the
premodern society are questioned and transformed.
Historical and statistical outlines are presented.
Selected modern industries are profiled. Trends
and implications are examined.

502. Matsumoto, Koji. Organizing for Higher
Productivity: An Analysis of Japanese Systems and
Practices. Tokyo: Asian Productivity
Organization, 1982.

The view is taken that productivity is the key to
social economic well-being. Japan´s success can
be a lesson to the U.S. Factors behind Japanese
productivity are studied. The statistics for
Japan are analyzed. Corporate structure and the
role of employees within the corporation are
examined. The identification of workers with the
company is explored, and the emphasis on
innovative management is treated. The role of the
government and the nature of the social
differentiation are analyzed as having a strong
impact on the general support of corporate
development. The pervasive character of
management is also noted.

503. Matsumura, Yutaka. Japan´s Economic Growth, 1945-
1960. Tokyo: Tokyo News Service, 1961.

The high productivity levels in Japan are the
result of a focused productivity drive. Its
results indicate that Japan´s levels of social and
economic well being are very high. Analysis of
Japan´s corporate structure is given. Its
management structure and the role of the employees
are described. Problems are identified. The
corporate environment is explored, including the
government-business relationship. Other factors
responsibile for high productivity are traced,
with special interest in the universality of the
Japanese management system.

504. Nakayama, Ichiro. Industrialization and Labor-
Management Relations in Japan. Tokyo: Japan
Institute of Labor, 1975.

This is a translation of a series of articles in
Japanese which represent the a consideration of
Japanese industrial relations. The social,
economic and political context of the industrial
relations system is traced. Postwar labor
developments during the period of rapid growth are
recounted. The assessment of Japanese traditions
and new challenges is made with a neoclassical
economics background, emphasizing the dynamics of
economics and politics.

505. Nishikawa, Shunsaku, ed. The Labor Market in
Japan: Selected Readings. Trans. Ross Mouer.
Tokyo: University of Tokyo Press (Distributed by
International Scholarly Book Services), 1980.

This collection contains descriptive essays on
Japanese behavior in the labor market, analysis of
statistical data, and methodological
investigations. Policy implications are also
drawn. The labor market is analyzed, with
treatment of the debates around the agriculture-
industry transformation, changes regarding the
work week and leisure, the effects of age and
education, and changes in the late 1970's. Wage
determination is also studied. The seniority
system, variations in starting wages, continuous
employment and its effects, conflicts and the
unions, and long-term trends are described.

506. Okochi, Kazuo, et al., eds. Workers and Employers
in Japan: The Japanese Employment Relations
System. Princeton, N.J.: Princeton University
Press, 1974.

This is a collaboration which discusses the system
by which the work force is managed in Japan,
especially in the modern sectors of industry. It
covers the institutions and structures operating
since 1970. The study offers some insights that
can be useful in the understanding of how changes
in norms can affect the management of workers in
other societies as well. Questions are raised
about the inevitability of industrialization and
whether the "convergence" hypothesis is born out,
as complex social forces tend to take on a common
pattern in all industrializing societies. Many of
these forces are outlined. The reorganization of
industrial relations in Japan is discussed, as
well as its legal framework. The labor market is
described. Top management and work organizations
are discussed in turn. Collective bargaining,
labor disputes, and the industrial reward system
are treated. Personnel administration and social
security are also examined. Conclusions are
offered as to the degree of change that has been

seen in the social system.

507. Ozawa, Terutomo. People and Productivity in
Japan. Work in America Institute Studies in
Productivity 25. New York: Pergamon Press, 1982.

This review of the literature covers English
language books which explore the reasons for
Japanese economic success. Growth in
productivity, industrial policy, technological
borrowing, dual industrial structure, and resource
transfers from agriculture to industry are
examined. The role of paternalism in management
is discussed, and the extent of paticipatory
management is outlined. Training patterns are
discussed, and future prospects are presented.

508. Roberts, Benjamin C., ed. Towards Industrial
Democracy: Europe, Japan & the United States.
Atlantic Institute for International Affairs
Research 2. Montclair, N.J.: Allanheld, Osmun &
Co. Publishers, Inc., 1979.

This book raises the issue of the legitimacy of
the authority of the business management in
Western nations, asking whether it is the
capitalist ownership principle or the assent of
the participating workers in the enterprise that
should prevail. Ideological changes offer the
possiblity of union-management decision making
based on collective and democratic procedures.
Yet there is a desire for both partners to
maintain autonomy, and to bargain in their self-
interest, restricting the role of the state in
acheiving the democratic consensus. One chapter
treats Japan´s experience, explaining the Joint
Management Committee´s role, the Joint
Consultative Committee, and recent trends and
reactions to European developments, with future
prospects.

509. Rohlen, Thomas P. For Harmony & Strength:
Japanese White-Collar Organization in
Anthropological Perspective. Center for Japanese
and Korean Studies. Berkeley: University of
California Press, 1974.

A large Japanese bank is studied from the point of
view of an anthropologist. Daily activities, from
personal conversations to bank ceremonies, are
observed and analyzed. The "language" of banking,
which includes the principles of the maximization
of returns, the supply and demand of the market,
and the like has its own logic. Yet in Japan,
these principles are used differently from the way
they are used in other countries. That difference

can be identified objectively through the
anthropological stance, while avoiding vague
references to the Japanese character or
traditions. The company's form, its ideology, and
the entrance and departure of members are
examined. The office group and hierarchy are
described. The bank's union, dormitories, and
marriage and the family are also treated.

510. Shetty, Y. Krishna, and Vernon M. Buehler, eds.
     Quality and Productivity Improvements: U.S. &
     Foreign Company Experiences. Chicago:
     Manufacturing Productivity Center, 1983.

     A product of the Utah State University, College of
     Business, this book offers several case studies on
     Japanese productivity, after general
     considerations on the nature and causes of
     productivity growth. Steel industries, the
     electric industry, and computer industry
     productivity are considered. Automobile industry
     productivity is also outlined. Some issues in the
     field of robotics are also raised, along with
     reflections on the post-industrial society.
     Guidelines for managerial action to improve
     productivity are given in conclusion.

511. Shigeyoshi, Tokunaga, and Joachim Bergmann, eds.
     Industrial Relations in Transition: The Cases of
     Japan and the Federal Republic of Germany.
     (Tokyo): University of Tokyo, 1984.

     A compilation of papers from the conference,
     "Industrial Relations in Transition," held at the
     Tohoku University, Sendai, September 1982, this
     book compares Japan and the Federal Republic of
     Germany. Conditions since the oil crisis of 1973
     have spelled the end of rapid growth, induced more
     resource conservation, and brought about
     stagflation. Technology growth has accelerated
     and unemployment has become endemic. These
     factors underly the industrial relations
     developments of economies today. Topics such as
     the labor market, managerial strategies, trade
     unions, and new technologies are offered.

512. Shirai, Taishiro, ed. Contemporary Industrial
     Relations in Japan. Madison, Wisconsin:
     University of Wisconsin Press, 1983.

     The aim of this collection is to present a
     balanced understanding of the complex Japanese
     industrial relations system. An attempt to dispel
     certain myths about the role of cultural factors
     as the chief determinant in the Japanese system is
     made. Another view, that of the backwardness of

the Japanese system, which is often held by the
many Japanese Marxists, is also presented, though
most of the contributors do not share it. Many
issues are raised, including the quality of life,
unionism and conflict resolution, public sector
relations, and management policies.

513. Taira, Koji. Economic Development & the Labor
     Market in Japan. Studies of the East Asian
     Institute Series. New York: Columbia University
     Press, 1970.

     This work on the Japanese labor force begins with
     an analytical section which concentrates on the
     various differentials in wages and their
     historical base. Changes in the structure of
     these differentials before and after the Second
     World War are explained. Then there is a
     treatment of the institutional aspects of the
     labor market in Japan. The origins of employer
     paternalism are traced, and the role of public
     policy in shaping the policies regarding labor is
     examined. The effect of unions on the wage
     structure and the shape of the labor market is
     also outlined. Finally there is a discussion of
     the political factors which shape the labor
     situation. Management practices and the
     participatory democracy of Japan are discussed.
     Conclusions regarding the significance of the
     labor market to the status of individual freedom
     in Japan are reached, and comments on the nation´s
     method of organized activity are made.

514. Takezawa, Shin´ichi, et al. Improvements in the
     Quality of Working Life in Three Japanese
     Industries. Geneva, (Switzerland): International
     Labour Office, 1982.

     In shipbuilding, electrical machinery, and
     automobile industries, the quality of working
     conditions are analyzed. Emphasis is placed on
     the improvements that were brought about by the
     joint efforts of unions and management. Workers´
     changing needs and aspirations are reflected in
     the study, and universal characteristics are
     identified which relate to work situations in
     other countries as well. Union-management study
     committees´ reports form the basis for the
     conclusions offered. Issues like the
     meaningfulness of work, the satisfaction of needs
     through compensation and the like are
     investigated.

515. Takezawa, Shin´ichi, and Arthur M. Whitehill.
     Work Ways, Japan and America. Tokyo: Japan
     Institute of Labor, 1981.

This book is the result of a survey research
project on the perceptions of factory workers in
the U.S. and Japan, taken in 1960 and 1976, to
discuss the implications of environmental changes
in the two countries during that time. The topics
considered include various aspects of working
life, such as the meaning of work, the acceptance
of work imperatives, the credibility of
management, worker-supervisor relations, shared
employment commitments, and employee assistance
and services. The materials are presented
systematically and with observations.

516. United States. Congress. Joint Economic Committee.
Subcommittee on International Trade, Finance, and
Security Economics. Japanese Productivity:
Lessons for America: Hearing Before the
Subcommittee on International Trade, Finance, and
Security Economics of the Joint Economic
Committee, Congress of the United States, Ninety-
Seventh Congress, First Session, November 4, 1981.
Washington, D.C.: G.P.O., 1982.

Testimony by a U.S. State Department official,
Robert D. Hormats is offered regarding problems in
U.S. productivity as compared to Japanese
performance. The lack of investment capital which
boosts productivity is cited as one of the key
elements. Robert B. Porter of the Department of
the Treasury discusses industrial productivity
trends and the U. S. case in particular. Richard
Cyert, President of Carnegie-Mellon University
discusses certain population trends in Japan as
contrasted with the U.S. The differences help to
explain the Japanese lead in robotics. David
LeVine, of Martin Marietta Corp., testifies about
his recent trip to Japan. Joseph Wright, Jr. of
the Commerce Department speaks about his
observations following a visit to Japan.

517. Wilburn, James R., ed. Productivity: A National
Priority. Malibu, Calif.: Pepperdine University
Press, 1982.

This volume is collection of speehes from a
conference sponsored by the Center for American
Private Enterprise at Pepperdine University and
the New American Foundation, in Sept., 1981.
Assumptions about American policy-making are
examined, and some ideological values of
individual freedom and private enterprise are
underscored. Japanese high productivity is
discussed, and Reaganomics is assessed.

518. Wilkinson, Thomas O. The Urbanization of Japanese
Labor, 1868-1955. Amherst, Mass: University of

Massachusetts Press, 1965.

Using demographic data to provide a sociological
perspective, this work gives a comprehensive
account of the urbanization process in Japan.
Some of the issues raised include the variations
in the urbanization pace and the reasons for them,
and the traits of the urbanizing population.
Industrialization and its forces are examined, and
the pattern in Japan is compared to the Western
pattern of urbanization. Also treated are themes
such as the location of urban centers, the role of
Meiji politics in industry, the rural traditions
which were maintained, and the unique position of
female labor.

519. Williamson, N. C. "Productivity: Another Japanese
     Export." Business: The Magazine of Managerial
     Thought and Action. 33.4 (Oct./Nov./Dec. 1983):
     3-10.

     The Japanese economy boasts a 10% increase in
     productivity for 1979 while the US productivity
     gains were only 2%. An important cause of the
     Japanese performance is the Provisional Plan for
     Corporate Democratization. This plan's aim is to
     set objectives for profit making, product quality
     and market share for designated industries. The
     role of the government in developing industries,
     with assessments of the optimum production growth
     for an industrial sector is discussed.

520. Woronoff, Jon. Japan's Wasted Workers. Tokyo:
     Lotus Press; Totwa, N. J.: Allenheld, Osmun, 1981,
     1983.

     Written for the Japanese public, this book
     outlines the dissatisfactions that are under the
     surface of the apparently smooth running Japanese
     labor-management "machine." Though the concept of
     lifetime employment was greeted with enthusiasm in
     the days when there were not enough workers to
     fill the needed places, nowadays there are many
     companies which would like to be able to do with
     fewer workers. And there are signs that young
     people do not want to "sign on" with the large
     companies. Their reluctance is part of a
     disillusionment which has many signs such as
     white-collar inefficiency, the placement of women
     in lower ranks, the narrowness of education, and
     defects in the management system itself.

AUTHORS AND EDITORS INDEX